Warmly Inscribed

Warmly Inscribed

THE NEW ENGLAND FORGER AND OTHER BOOK TALES

LAWRENCE
AND
NANCY GOLDSTONE

THOMAS DUNNE BOOKS
ST. MARTIN'S PRESS
NEW YORK

THOMAS DUNNE BOOKS.
An imprint of St. Martin's Press.

www.stmartins.com

Library of Congress Cataloging-in-Publication Data

Goldstone, Lawrence.
    Warmly inscribed : the New England forger and other book tales /
Lawrence and Nancy Goldstone.
        p. cm.
    ISBN 0-312-26268-X
    1. Goldstone, Lawrence, 1947–.   2. Goldstone, Nancy Bazelon.
3. Book collectors—United States—Biography.   4. Book collecting—
United States—Anecdotes.   5. Antiquarian booksellers—United
States—Anecdotes.   I. Goldstone, Nancy Bazelon.   II. Title.

    Z989 .G65 2001
    002'.075—dc21

                                                            2001017496

First Edition: June 2001

10   9   8   7   6   5   4   3   2   1

For Emily, who always has good taste in books,
and
Darwin, to whom books always taste good

Contents

1

THE LIBRARY OF CONGRESS:
114,000,000 BOOKS, SO LITTLE TIME
1

2

THE INCOMPARABLE MAX
46

3

THE NEW ENGLAND FORGER
78

4

INTO THE TEETH OF THE FLORIDA BOOK WORLD
132

5

BOOKS@PROFIT.COM
161

6

BOOKING THE TREND
180

7

AFTERWORD
204

Chapter 1

The Library of Congress: 114,000,000 Books, So Little Time

Almost from the moment we became interested in old books, we wanted to take a bibliophile's holiday to Washington, D.C. We had heard that there were lots of outstanding and unusual shops in a relatively small area, and, of course, the nation's capital is the home of the Library of Congress, a place that neither of us had visited and that we knew little about.

We had been to Washington the previous spring but that had been a family trip. We had taken Emily, then seven, and done what all parents do—gone to the Lincoln Memorial (twice), waited two hours to ascend to the top of the Washington Monument, fought our way through a solid wall of other families at the Air and Space Museum, and even procured a congressional tour of the Capitol. All of these activities had been punctuated by visits to the cafeteria at the American History Museum (famous the world over for its macaroni and cheese) and two rides on the carousel every time we crisscrossed the mall (which was frequently).

We had gone to some relatively untrammeled places as well. We sat for about fifteen minutes in James McNeill Whistler's Peacock

Room at the Freer, stopped at the Greenville lunch counter, site of the first civil rights sit-in, and admired Albert Bierstadt's *Last of the Buffalo* at the Corcoran Museum of Art. We all had a terrific time and Emily decided that Washington was her favorite city on earth.

But there had been no books and not a single visit to a bookstore, so we had promised ourselves that we would come back soon, just the grown-ups, stay at a hip hotel in Georgetown instead of the Embassy Suites, and concentrate on books. We would even eat in restaurants specializing in neither macaroni and cheese nor spaghetti with butter.

It turned out, however, that coming back to Washington without Emily was not going to be all that easy.

"Mommy and Daddy have to go on business. It's only for a couple of days."

No reply from our daughter. Just a wrinkled forehead and the look of stupendous hurt that she had perfected by watching our six-month-old beagle puppy, Darwin.

"It won't be fun for you," we insisted soothingly. "We're going to be spending a lot of time in bookstores."

"I like bookstores," said Emily.

"We'll be talking to people . . . sometimes for hours. You'll have to be quiet for *hours*. You can't tell us you're tired. You can't tell us you're hungry. We'll be working. You'll just have to sit there and amuse yourself."

"Okay."

"And we're not going to Italian restaurants every night. You'll have to try new food. No spaghetti."

"What if they have spaghetti on the menu?" asked Emily.

"If they have spaghetti on the menu, that'll be okay."

"Most places have spaghetti on the menu," said Emily knowingly.

"Well, if we take you out of school for a couple of days, we're going to ask your teacher to give you an assignment. You'll have to work too."

"Maybe I can do a report."

The deal we finally cut was for an extended Columbus Day weekend. Thursday, Friday, and part of Saturday would be for books (although Emily could go on the carousel if we happened to pass by); the rest of Saturday, all of Sunday, and Monday morning were hers. *Our* itinerary was: the Library of Congress on Thursday afternoon; the Folger Shakespeare Library Friday morning; Capitol-area book dealers Friday afternoon; and Georgetown bookstores Saturday morning. Emily's choices were the Supreme Court, Ford's Theater, reading the Gettysburg Address and the Second Inaugural at the Lincoln Memorial, the National Zoo, and the dinosaurs and the Hope diamond at the natural history museum. She had, in fact, been assigned to write a report on the trip by her third-grade teacher.

So, on the Thursday morning before Columbus Day, we hopped on the shuttle and, by twelve-thirty, we were all checked into what seemed to be our old room at the Embassy Suites in Old Town Alexandria.

There are issues involved with taking Emily on a trip that go beyond buying a third ticket and making sure there's an extra bed in the hotel room. For example, there is the question of, "Who can I take with me?" Emily has an extensive collection of stuffed animals, each of which (whom?) has a name, a distinct personality, a speaking voice, and a birthday that is entered yearly on our wall calendar. Among the choices were: Mr. Bear, who has been with her since birth; Tyrannosaurus; Whalie (excluded immediately—too big); and Dolphina (see Whalie). Then there's Little Bear, Travel Bear, Bearin (with the angel's wings), Big Bear (too Big), Flamingeay and Yonder (the Happy Couple—they're married), Brownie, Gorilla, Floppy Dog, Sandy, Snakeus, Chickerin, Sheepish, Pragen the Penguin, and last, but not least, Bearite, a gift from Mommy under extremely trying circumstances (read: immense sentimental value). After extensive discussions as to number and size, Emily settled on Mr. Bear, Little Bear, Travel Bear, and Bearite. (Bear with us. This has great significance later in the chapter.)

We quickly unpacked, opened Emily's fold-out bed, tucked in all four little bears, and set off to meet the rare-book librarian at the Library of Congress.

The Library of Congress was to be the centerpiece of the trip, at least from our end. It wasn't simply that we hadn't been there before—we had no idea how big the Library actually was, or how many people worked there, or how they divided the responsibility, or even who the Librarian of Congress was. We had developed this Dickensian vision of a dark, musty, forbidding building populated by a staff of ancient, unsmiling, long-fingernailed Uriah Heeps, one of whom would grudgingly disappear into the stacks for hours before returning with some dingy tome that he or she would extend our way but refuse to let us touch or even see the inside of without five letters of recommendation from Nobel laureates.

Nonetheless, we had hoped to get an appointment with *somebody,* so about two weeks before the trip, we called the main number and told the operator that we wrote about old books. The operator put us on to the public relations department, and the public relations department put us on to someone named Mark Dimunation.

"Hi. My name is Nancy Goldstone. My husband Larry and I write books about books. Are you the Librarian of Congress?"

"No, the Librarian of Congress is James H. Billington."

"Can I talk to him?" Mark sounded much too young to be anybody important.

"No, he doesn't usually talk to people. He's too busy."

"Can I talk to you?"

"Sure."

"Who are you?"

"I'm the head of the Rare Book and Special Collections Division," said Mark. "The Library is divided into different divisions. There's Prints and Photographs, Music, Manuscripts, Motion Pictures. . . ."

"Well, we're coming to Washington and we want to visit the Library and see some of the rare books."

"What did you want to see?" asked Mark.

We had read up a little bit on the Library before we called. "Can we see the rough draft of the Declaration of Independence or the Gettysburg Address?"

"Those are both manuscripts," Mark pointed out gently. "They're in the Manuscript Division. They usually don't like to trot them out for individual visitors. However, you're in luck. As it turns out, the rough draft of the Declaration of Independence is on exhibition right now."

"Well, what if you choose some books that you like? We'd be very interested in whatever you think is special."

"I suppose I could do that. When do you want to come in?"

"What if we come by at three o'clock Thursday?"

"Well, we close at five," said Mark. "You're only giving me two hours? We have one hundred and fourteen million books."

One hundred and fourteen million were a lot of books, so we got there at two.

There are three buildings that make up the Library of Congress— the Jefferson, the Madison, and the Adams. The Madison and the Adams are two giant granite rectangles, just the kind of buildings where you'd expect to find all those books. The Jefferson, the main building, is the oldest of the three. Completed in 1896, it's across the street from the front of the Capitol. (It's the back of the Capitol that faces the mall.) It's a huge white-stone structure with tall arched windows, columns, a dome, and lots of personality. This is where we were to meet Mark Dimunation.

As we walked up to the front entrance, we came upon a tremendous fountain, replete with thickly muscled, bare-breasted women on charging horses, guys drinking from squirting seashells, and a Charles Atlas–like figure in the center. This, as we later read in the brochure, was the Court of Neptune fountain. The men were Neptune and his son Triton and the naked lady wrestlers were sea nymphs. Some nymphs. On the building itself were busts of Mark Twain, Benjamin Franklin, and other notables whom we couldn't quite recognize.

Behind the fountain was a wide staircase that led up to a set of enormous doors under the statues. (Washington is a great city, but everything seems built on the scale of a Leni Riefenstahl film.) These doors are no longer used, however, so visitors are directed to the carriage entrance, a set of much smaller doors under the stairs.

Mark met us in the lobby, just outside a Tel Aviv Airport–caliber security gate. He was in his forties—not as young as he sounded on the phone, but still pretty young, it seemed to us, for a job like this. He was tall and lean, with short, modishly cut hair, and wore a dark blue suit with a bright blue shirt and patterned tie. When he shook our hands, he was formal and friendly at the same time. Then he looked past us, unsure about Emily, like an actor who had been warned never to work with children or animals. Certainly, there must have been few occasions when he had been called upon to escort an eight-year-old through a collection of priceless rare books.

"The Library of Congress is actually the *library* of *Congress*," he said as we walked through the metal detector. The second he began to speak, his enthusiasm for the Library was evident. "There are rooms, in fact, reserved for members of the House and Senate or their staffs to use as they like, usually for research on some pending question such as arms control or health care. We're connected to the congressional office buildings by tunnels underneath. That's why the security is so high here. We are technically an entrance to Congress."

Mark was originally from Minnesota, and as an undergrad attended St. Olaf's College. He was going for his Ph.D. in eighteenth-

and nineteenth-century American history at Berkeley when, to make a little money, he got a job in the university library cataloging rare books. He ended up switching his major to library science and working there all through his graduate years.

"Next thing I knew, I had a career," he said.

He spent twenty years at other libraries, including those at Stanford and Cornell, before getting the job here two years ago.

"Back then, most people got into this like I did—they kind of backed into it," he said. "Today it's much more specialized. More people are studying specifically to work with special collections."

Before we went upstairs to the Great Hall, Mark showed us the Gershwin room, where Gershwin's grand piano stood on a raised island in the center surrounded by a waist-high glass partition. Ira's typewriter sat on a desk to the side and the walls were filled with framed photographs, playbills, and other memorabilia. Generally the Library had music playing but the room was currently under-going some maintenance, so now it was silent. We went across the hall to the Coolidge Auditorium, which sat perhaps five hundred people and had such remarkable acoustics that when a man walked across the stage about one hundred feet away, the click of his shoes on the wood floor was crisp, like the sound of a twig cracking in a deserted forest.

When we were back outside, everything began to echo once more and the contrast was startling. Mark got a sneaky little grin on his face, like a small boy about to let you see his secret worm collection.

"Now we can really start," he said. "Let's go up to the Great Hall."

The Library of Congress was founded in 1800 when Congress appropriated five thousand dollars "for the purchase of such books as may be necessary for the use of Congress . . . and for fitting up a suitable apartment [in the Capitol itself] for containing them and for placing them therein."

Book and apartment prices were obviously much lower then, but cheap or not, the whole thing turned out to be moot when, near the end of the War of 1812, the British came by and burned down the Capitol and the Library along with it. Perhaps it was fate, though, because what the nation got the second time around was so much better—not only an extraordinary library, but also a timeless vision of books and learning sprung from one of the greatest minds of the time.

Those books and that vision belonged, of course, to Thomas Jefferson. Believing firmly that liberty and learning were inseparable, Jefferson offered his personal library to Congress in 1815 to replace the books burned by the British and seed a new collection. A voracious reader and collector himself, Jefferson had accumulated a library of nearly sixty-five hundred books in a variety of languages and covering a wide diversity of subjects. At the time, it was the largest personal book collection in the United States.

You'd think that Congress would have snapped up such an offer, but it turned out that there was an intense debate. Jefferson was interested in so many things—architecture, cooking, philosophy, science, farming, astronomy—and some congressmen thought that cookbooks, for example, weren't exactly necessary in a congressional library, particularly since some of them weren't even in English. And then, of course, there was the additional fact that Jefferson was not offering his collection for free. Still, Jefferson argued that the Library of Congress should reflect the same universality as his library on the grounds that there is no subject or book that might not be helpful in the formation of the nation's laws. Eventually Congress, grumbling all the way, accepted this approach and paid Jefferson twenty-four thousand dollars for his collection and the Library of Congress was reestablished.

"Universality was Jefferson's philosophy and now it is his legacy," said Mark as we climbed marble stairs. "He structured his library partly based on Bacon's organization of knowledge and partly on Diderot's tree, with subjects branching off a main trunk. He divided the books into three categories: memory, reason, and imagination.

"Today, the collection goes way beyond books and manuscripts. Over five thousand people work for the Library of Congress. We're the conduit for smaller libraries. Our map collection is unsurpassed. We have film, music, musical instruments, prints, photographs. We have collections in every language and distribute our cataloging to the Anglo-American world. We even have a department of lesser-known languages."

He stopped at the landing, and then, with a sweep of his arm, announced, "This is the Great Hall!"

People often gasp when they walk into the Capitol rotunda, but the rotunda is a shack compared to the Great Hall. Rising up two stories, the hall is framed by marble pillars and archways. The walls are decorated with murals and statues and frescoes and quotations appropriate to books and wisdom and learning. The floors, also of marble, are inlaid with intricate patterns. There is gold leaf everywhere. The hall is topped by a dome, done seemingly in silver, which picks up some of the pattern from the floor and is ringed by a circle of painted figures.

Whoever designed this really knew their stuff—ornate as it all is, it's still tasteful. Just a whisper more and it could easily have looked like a brothel. We all stopped and stared, and Emily, who had been frantically writing in her notebook trying to get down everything Mark said for her report, dropped to her knees, the better to scribble her notes.

"No genuflecting in the Great Hall," he told her.

"Those figures ringing the very top are portraits of Francis Bacon, Aristotle, Goethe, Shakespeare, Molière, Moses, and Herodotus," Mark continued. "People had wondered for years why they would do gold leaf all the way up the sides and then change to the much more pedestrian silver at the very top. It was only after the building was restored that we realized that what was really at the top, was, in 1897, the most valuable metal on earth. Can you guess what it was?"

"Platinum?"

"Nope. It's aluminum. Aluminum leaf," he said.

"They did the ceiling in Reynolds Wrap?"

"Kind of," said Mark. "At the time, the refining process was so expensive that it made aluminum the most valuable metal on earth, so that's what they used.

"We're standing in one of the last great temples of books. The entire Jefferson Building and especially this hall tell a very large story about the history of communication. It breaks it down into families, oral tradition, the march of civilization, on to printing, and the glory of American civilization up to the end of the nineteenth century. Around the windows, you'll see printers' marks, slogans, muses . . . it was done right after the Chicago World's Fair. That's how they got all the artisans together in one place. It was one of the first buildings to be fully electrified. In fact, the whole place is kind of a celebration of the lightbulb. Look. All the lights, even in the fanciest chandeliers, are naked lightbulbs. It seems modern now."

It was true. There were lines of lightbulbs, circles of lightbulbs, and patterns of lightbulbs, all with clear glass and visible filaments. It looked like a giant display at Restoration Hardware.

Mark took us through a doorway closed to the public and showed us the members' rooms, furnished in deep reds, with wood paneling and inlaid gold. These rooms were every bit the match of J. Pierpont Morgan's reading room in New York. For all their complaining about government spending, congressmen certainly don't scrimp on appropriations for themselves. Then we returned to the Great Hall, where Mark stopped at the marble staircase.

"I love this part," he said. "See the putti?" There were marble cherubs carved along the railing. "Our putti don't get to frolic like European cherubs. Our putti have to work, and they all work very hard. See? There's a baby printer, a laborer . . . the Jefferson Building is one of the finest examples of overall decoration. The architectural tour here is fascinating."

We walked up the stairs to what was either a smaller hall or a giant alcove. On either side was a large, dark-wood, glass-fronted sealed case.

"This is just a coincidence," he said, "but it's one of those great coincidences. All around us on the walls is the mural of communication, starting with oral communication and ending with Gutenberg and the invention of movable type. But it's the two cases that mark one of the great transitions of civilization." He took us to the case on the right first. There was a huge, beautifully rendered book at least two feet high. "This is the giant Bible of Mainz," he said. "It was done in about 1453. It's a manuscript Bible. You can see how carefully the scribes drew the lines. This is one of the last great manuscript books. It's part of the Lessing J. Rosenwald Collection."

Then we walked back across to the case on the left, in which was displayed another large book in utterly pristine condition. "And this, of course, is the forty-two-line Gutenberg Bible. It's one of three known to have been printed on vellum and it's in perfect condition. So, here you have in the same city, in Mainz, one or two years apart, two magnificent Bibles, one effectively the last of its kind, the other the first."

We had seen a Gutenberg Bible at the Pierpont Morgan Library, which at the time we thought was in remarkable condition for a book 550 years old. But here at the Library of Congress was one that might have been printed yesterday.

"You know the apocryphal story, of course," Mark continued. "They say that when Fust, Gutenberg's partner, brought two of these new printed Bibles to Paris, the cardinal held them up and screamed, 'This is the Devil's work! Only Satan would make two books exactly the same!'"

We went up another small flight of stairs and through a door that led out to a small platform high above the Main Reading Room. There was a Plexiglas partition that separated this small public area from the rest of the room. Even after everything we had seen, the Main Reading Room was perhaps the most magnificent of all. It was circular, at least four stories high and more than thirty yards in diameter. There was a large circulation desk in the center, with rows of desks ringing concentrically outward toward the far wall. The wall, at least at ground level, was entirely devoted to bookshelves.

"The books in this room are all reference," said Mark. "The actual books are either in the other buildings or underground in this one. There are dumbwaiters hidden in the circulation desk and a series of conveyer belts under the street that leads to the stacks. With one hundred and fourteen million books, the system, as you might suspect, is pretty extensive.

"You have to be a registered reader to work in this room but becoming a registered reader is pretty easy. Anyone who has a legitimate academic purpose and two letters of recommendation can become one."

As we left, Mark looked at his watch. It was almost four o'clock. "We have to get moving," he said. "But before we go to the rare-book department, you've got to at least see the public exhibit."

We were already bug-eyed and Emily had written page after page in laborious third-grade print and her hand was about falling off, but Mark was already leading us to another room and an exhibit in glass display cases called American Treasures of the Library of Congress.

Just inside, an old video of Groucho Marx being interviewed by Johnny Carson was playing on a small television screen. The Library had apparently asked Groucho to leave his papers to the nation. Groucho, the man who said, "I will not join any club who would have me as a member," had found this to be a source of great amusement.

"As you can see," Mark said with a smile, gesturing at Groucho, "Jefferson's concept of universality is well represented in this room."

He led us to the right, to a case that held a letter from Thomas Jefferson outlining his thoughts on libraries, as well as a copy of *The Federalist Papers.*

"This was Jefferson's copy. See? He identified which essay was written by Hamilton, which by Madison, and which by John Jay."

Further inside, in another case, we saw an exhibit of the contents of Abraham Lincoln's pockets on the night he was killed.

"Okay," said Mark, after we'd had a minute or two to look. "Let's go to the Rare Book Division."

LJ 239
Rare Book and
Special Collections
Division
And Reading Room

The Rare Book Reading Room wasn't as grand as other areas of the Library we'd seen. It looked a bit like a converted courtroom, with the librarians' area in the front separated by a swinging gate from a lot of long tables, each with a researcher or two poring over a book or pamphlet. Most of the researchers were young. Mark told us that, with only a handful of exceptions, an accredited researcher could use anything in the library.

"We have eight hundred thousand rare books," he said. "We define a rare book, more or less, as anything printed before 1800. It's higher for American printing—hovers around 1826." He pointed toward the walls at the end of the room. There was a nondescript-looking door in either corner. "The vault runs four stories up one side, across the ceiling, and four stories down the other side. It's a mimic of Independence Hall. Readers come in and register with us, we take down their requests, and the material is brought to them. The material cannot leave the room. Before we go into the vault, let's go across the hall."

He got a key and took us to a large room opposite the reading room. Inside were wraparound floor-to-ceiling bookshelves filled with books.

"This is the Lessing J. Rosenwald room. Remember downstairs—he gave us the Mainz Bible. Rosenwald was from Main Line Philadelphia and the founder of Sears, Roebuck. He was interested in the history of illustration and printing and he left us his collection. The room we are in is a replica of Rosenwald's own reference library with the original furniture. This was his couch, his library table . . . all the furniture and reference books are his. And remember," Mark added as we looked around at the hundreds and hundreds of books, "these are just the reference books. The rare books are in the vault.

"Rosenwald captured most of the great moments in the history of printing," he went on. "Moreover, he was enormously concerned with quality. He bought most of his books in the 1930s and 1940s from Rosenbach—they say that the second-highest day of expenditure in the Rosenbach shop's history was the day Lessing J. Rosenwald walked in. In addition to the giant Bible, he gave us ten block books, all in excellent condition. Can you imagine? Ten block books. Nobody has ten block books."

(Block printing was a precursor of movable type. Ink was applied to a woodblock, part of which had been cut away, leaving only a desired text or design in relief, then pressed onto a fabric or paper to produce an image. This was the first method of producing multiple images from one master copy, although obviously the master could not be used for anything else afterwards.

Block printing may have begun in India in the fifth century B.C. and was used extensively in China four or five hundred years before it was introduced in Europe in the thirteenth century. It became a popular book-printing technique in Germany in the late fourteenth and early fifteenth centuries, until Gutenberg sent block books the way of eight-track stereo tapes.)

Mark actually sighed. "The Rosenwald is just a great collection. We simply don't have many of those great, classic fifteenth-century collections anymore. There's the Mellon Collection, which might come to the National Gallery, and there are some strong Romantic collections. But these days, most collections are more subject oriented. You're much more likely to see a collection on the history of technology, or the history of psychology, than on the history of illustrated books.

"It makes things a little difficult because, since we are very strong in so many areas, the kind of collection we go after is necessarily more defined. It's our job to build on our cultural heritage—the cultural memory of early America. So we're always looking to fill in the gaps, to build on the comprehensiveness of the collection. For example, we have no comprehensive collection of American printing.

"But what we do have is extraordinary. We have an amazing Lincoln and Civil War collection—Confederate newspapers, publications, pamphlets. Did you know that towards the end of the war the South ran out of paper and had to use wallpaper? There's this one newspaper we have, the entire paper had already been set to be published, and the Union Army was right on the outskirts of the town. And the people of the town had written in the newspaper that Grant would be dining on fricassee of kitten, meaning that the Yankees would never take the town and they'd starve trying. Then, of course, the Union came into the town and found the newspaper—the Confederates had all fled—and the Yankees reset it, calling it the commemorative edition. Everything was left the same except in the corner they wrote that General Grant was dining in town and the Confederates were eating fricassee of kitten.

"And when you turned the paper over," said Mark, "you could see the floral pattern because it was printed on wallpaper.

"Two separate Walt Whitman collections came into the Library at about the same time, and it led to another one of those marvelous coincidences. In one of the collections, there was a copy of *Leaves of Grass* with Henry David Thoreau's signature inside. In the other was a copy of a book by Thoreau with Whitman's signature. But that one also had an inscription saying, 'I saw Henry David Thoreau on the docks in Brooklyn. I gave him my copy of *Leaves of Grass* and he gave me this.'

"Imagine, a great moment like that . . . Thoreau and Whitman just happening to meet on the docks in Brooklyn and exchanging books . . . and we can reconstruct it because it comes to us in two separate collections." Mark sighed once more. "It's wonderful, isn't it?

"We have so many other things too. We have an early school grammar that belonged to Abraham Lincoln. He studied it over and over again. At the same time he was courting a young woman—she died, but before that, while he was still seeing her, he gave her the book, and between the lines of the title page he wrote as a kind of joke: 'Jane X is now studying grammar.'

"We have tens of thousands of broadsides, tens of thousands of pamphlets. It becomes a very complicated business. We don't keep everything we get. We're not a copyright library. Selection is made. Not every auto repair book is retained. Literature has never been a big strength. Having said that, we have one of the great twentieth-century collections.

"We buy material from the fifteenth century to the present. We have ongoing acquisition projects. The Harlem Renaissance, for example. We look for research-level quality materials. We look for women authors, like Harriet Beecher Stowe. We only have first editions. We're looking to document the North American Women's Suffrage Movement. First and foremost, we are a research library. We're looking to build a certain depth, especially in American history. We're trying to document the American experience; we're looking to represent groups not ordinarily represented and to document cultural trends and political issues such as temperance. We look for things that do it for you with a single moment. For example, a ballooning collection—it documents cultural activity as much as it is part of the history of aviation.

"But it's harder to buy things now—there's more competition. Everything is done by auction, and we're competing with other libraries—university collections and big collectors."

Still, with all the treasures, it is Thomas Jefferson who is most revered.

"Fire is kind of a tradition here," said Mark. "First the British did it when they burned the Capitol. Then the Library burned again in 1851—we lost two-thirds of Jefferson's books.

"Millicent Sowerby put together a five-volume bibliography of the books that Jefferson apparently sold to the Library of Congress in 1815. We've identified every volume we still hold. In addition, we've identified two to three thousand books in matching edition—that is, they're the exact same edition that Jefferson had. We're down to six hundred and seventeen matching editions that we are still looking for.

"What makes it so challenging is that we will only take the precise edition that Jefferson actually owned, and Jefferson was a secondhand-book buyer. He used book jobbers. He wasn't a bibliophile in the sense of first editions in great condition. If he wanted the book, he got it. If it happened to be the fourth Dublin edition, so be it. So now we've got to find the book in the fourth Dublin edition, and that's a big job."

Even working every day in the midst of all of this, there are still some things that stand out.

"The day I saw the copy of the Declaration of Independence, and then I found out it was Washington's copy, the one he read to the troops, that he actually handled that document . . . the day I walked up and down the aisle of the Rosenwald Collection and realized there were so many books I knew of that I had never handled . . . the day I was in the stacks looking for something and I turned around and suddenly realized I was looking at books from the Tsar's Imperial Collection . . . the time I saw books from the Third Reich Collection."

Mark checked his watch once more. "Oh my God," he said, "you haven't even seen any books yet! Let's get your stuff from the cloakroom and go to the vault."

After we'd retrieved our coats and backpacks, we went back and left them in the Rare Book Reading Room. Mark signed for a serious-looking key and led us to the door at the far left-hand corner of the room. When he led us through, we saw an equally serious-looking security system on the wall.

"We have to be out of here by five," Mark said. "We turn security over to the Capitol Police, and they don't like it when people are in the vault after hours."

When the door closed behind us, we found ourselves standing in an aisle so narrow that only Emily could walk through without brushing her shoulders. There were metal shelves up and back, and we realized that we had just been locked in a vault with well over a billion dollars worth of books.

Mark took us to one of the shelves nearest the door. "These books have been identified as part of the one-third that remains of the original collection that Jefferson sold to Congress in 1815. Jefferson did not as a rule write very much in his books. He had no bookplate, no name in the book, none of the obvious things, so I'll bet you're wondering how we know that these books are his."

He took out a small red leather-bound book from the top shelf. "It has a dead giveaway," he said, and then opened to a page at the beginning. He smiled and leaned down.

"See, Emily, how the pages of the book are lettered as well as numbered at the bottom? *A*1, *A*2, *B*1, *B*2? They didn't print the books in order in those days, they printed them in sections, and in order to know how to sew the sections together, they alphabetized them. When it came to the *I*s—they didn't use *J*s—Thomas Jefferson would very lightly turn the *I* into a *J* and put a *T* in front of it."

Emily hadn't said a word in two hours. It was perhaps the best behaved she'd ever been in her entire life. Now, with Mark Dimunation, the rare-book librarian at the Library of Congress, showing her a book from Thomas Jefferson's personal library, a huge smile erupted on her face and her eyes went wider than if we had just offered her a lifetime supply of hot fudge sundaes. It was as proud and as happy as we had ever seen her. From that moment on, Mark showed everything to Emily first, us second.

Mark leafed to a page in the middle. There were "*TJ1*," "*TJ2*," and so on, almost like the work of a schoolboy.

"Then, when it came to the *Ts*, he'd put a *J* after each. Doesn't it just make you *like* this man?" asked Mark. He got a very happy, boyish look on his face before he put the book away.

The second book he took out was Jefferson's copy of a book originally owned by Benjamin Franklin. Unlike Jefferson, Franklin wrote in his books. Copiously. Jefferson must have recognized the handwriting and bought the book from a secondhand-book dealer. It was two pamphlets stitched together, both published in England by authors enumerating all of the reasons why the American colonies did not deserve independence.

We could almost see Franklin sitting in a big comfortable chair in his study, furiously scribbling his reactions to the Tories' arguments. The handwriting was very precise and every word was legible. At one point, when the writer was proselytizing extensively about some point or other, Franklin wrote, "Oh get on with it already." At the end of the second pamphlet, Franklin jotted down his overall conclusions. It was something to the effect that this was a very nice young man, who obviously believed strongly in his views; it was a shame that he was an idiot.

"Would you like to see the world's tiniest elevator?" asked Mark.

We left the Jefferson Collection and squeezed into the elevator, which had the dimensions of a good-sized pencil box, and took it two floors.

"This is the Rosenwald Collection," he said. "Have you ever seen a block book?"

When we assured him that we had not, Mark took a large, heavy brown tome from the shelf.

"This is from 1456," he said, unhooking two clamps opposite the spine, which held the book closed. "That's a year after Gutenberg so it doesn't seem that this was really a transition between manuscripts and type set as we originally thought."

"Would you like to touch this?" he asked Emily

She delicately reached out a finger and touched the cover.

"What does it feel like?"

"Like a piece of wood," Emily said.

"That's right," he said. "They didn't make books back then the way they do now. They stacked the pages and placed them between two blocks of wood. Then they punched holes all the way through." He opened the cover and pointed to a spot at the spine, covered over with paper, where the book appeared to have been bound. "If you touch right there, you can feel the hole.

"Then they took string and ran it through the holes, pulled it very, very tight, and that's how the book was bound. Do you see the clamps on the outside? Can you guess what they were for?"

"To keep the book together, so it didn't fall apart?" Emily offered.

"That's very close. These books were kept in monasteries where it was damp and cold. The clamps are there to keep the books tightly shut so that they don't absorb moisture and expand. There were times when books on a shelf expanded so much that eventually one of them would shoot out of the bookshelf. There are instances of monks being killed by flying books."

Mark opened the book to a page in the center. "Do you know how these pages were made? They cut images into blocks of wood, put ink on the surface, then pressed the block onto the page." He leafed through the book until he came to a page depicting what appeared to be a large cauldron with a hideous, large-fanged beast at either end and a lot of really unhappy-looking people being par-boiled in the center.

Mark turned to us. "This is the 'Devil's Mouth,'" he said. "I wanted to use it for the staff Christmas card . . . you know, greetings from the Library of Congress . . . but they wouldn't let me. I thought it showed character but, I suppose, as my father said, you can have too much character."

He closed the block book, returned it to the shelf, and took out another volume a little ways away. "This is a book of hours, done in a famous workshop in 1524." He opened to a page in the center. "This is called an illuminated manuscript," he said to Emily. "What do you think?"

The page had an illustration of an angel floating over a tree; the colors were so pure that they leapt off the page. We had seen illuminated manuscripts before, but never anything in quite this fine a condition. The detail in the leaves and in the halo was astounding.

"The fine lines were done with brushes of a single hair," said Mark.

We looked through the book of hours for a few minutes, and then Mark asked, "Do you want to see my favorite book?" We could hear the door opening and closing under us. "They must be wondering what we're doing," he said. "We have to close up and give the keys to the police." He hurried to the next aisle and took out a very large book in a custom sleeve.

He opened it to a random page. On the left side of the book was a column of figures, like the stock market quotations they print in the business section of the newspaper. On the opposing page were cutout wheels laid one on top of the other, so you could spin them around like a dial. It looked almost like a child's game.

"This is an astronomy book from 1540 done by Peter Apian—he was usually known as Petrus Apianus. You use the dials to find the numbers you need. Then you go to the column on the left and find those numbers and it will tell you where you are anywhere in the world. Isn't it amazing? So intricate."

In many ways, a nation is known by what it chooses to protect. With all of the clamoring by so many vested interests for their share of public funds and by other interests for a reduction of the public funds for there to be a share of, it gave us a deep feeling of national pride to know that our country values this monument to humanity's constant drive for self-improvement enough to maintain the Library of Congress in all its splendor. We know this sounds corny, but we defy anyone to visit this awesome, incredible building and not feel the same way.

We left just as the Library was closing. We were so proud of Emily for her exemplary behavior over three hours that we managed to go by the carousel and squeeze in multiple rides before it (a) began to rain and (b) they closed it down for the night. Then we got back on the Metro (the only way to travel in D.C.), took the ride back to Alexandria, and went out to dinner at a lethal Italian restaurant (not to be named). Emily got spaghetti with tomato sauce. We got diarrhea.

The next morning, bright and early, chipper and a little bit thinner, we all headed for the Folger Shakespeare Library.

The Folger was a gift to the nation from Henry Clay Folger and his wife, Emily Jordan Folger. While a student at Amherst, Folger paid twenty-five cents to attend a lecture on Shakespeare by Ralph Waldo Emerson and was inspired afterwards to go out and buy a cheap set of Shakespeare's works. From that modest purchase sprang a lifelong obsession. While many collectors are victims of lifelong obsessions, not too many of them become chairman of the board of Standard Oil as a means to support it. He and Emily, who had no children, spent the last thirty years of their lives amassing their collection.

(This reminded us of another great collector with the same initials and a similar name, Henry Clay Frick. Frick, of course, en-

dowed the Frick Museum in New York City. He owned not only
one of the great private art collections in the world, but also one of
the great collections of art books. The museum is located in Frick's
town house on Madison Avenue and 71st Street.

What nobody talks about is that this is the very same Henry
Clay Frick who was running the Carnegie Steel Company plant in
Homestead, Pennsylvania, in 1892, during one of the bloodiest
strikes in the nation's history. Frick, who didn't seem to mind that
those who worked in the plant toiled under conditions that could
generously be described as inhuman while not making enough
money to keep their children much above a starvation level, actually
ordered a wage cut. When the workers' fledgling union responded
by calling a strike, Frick brought in three hundred Pinkerton detectives to run the plant. There were riots and a near war between the
workers and the Pinkertons. Almost twenty people died and scores
were injured. Frick was so reviled by the working class that Emma
Goldman persuaded her lover, Alexander Berkman, to travel from
New York to Pittsburgh to kill him. Berkman, posing as a contractor selling scab labor, got to see Frick at a newspaper office. He
walked in and shot Frick twice and then stabbed him twice in the
legs. Frick survived and was back at work in a month while Berkman went to jail for twenty years. Frick subsequently brought in the
National Guard and succeeded in breaking both the strike and the
union.

While the Frick Collection—like the Folger—is magnificent
and we have no idea of labor relations in Folger's Standard Oil, it
doesn't hurt to remember occasionally where the money for some
of these great collections came from.)

"The Folgers were actually pretty boring people," said Richard
Kuhta, the Folger's librarian. "They had a modest house on Long
Island, they didn't entertain or go out much—they weren't part of
the great social whirl."

Kuhta, a trim, intense man, has been at the Folger for five years.

We were sitting in his office, an Elizabethan-looking room that was furnished with tables from the early seventeenth century. A genuine Shakespearean-era textile hung on the wall.

"The Folgers were part of the golden period of collecting in America," he continued. "That was 1880–1930. The big names were Morgan, Huntington, Newberry, and Folger.

"The Folgers collected literature from the period 1475 to 1640, when the Globe Theatre was closed by Cromwell. It was from Caxton to Dryden—it's a peerless collection. Then, in 1938, the Folger Library bought the collection of Sir Lester Harmsworth. Harmsworth was from a newspaper family in England. He collected everything *but* literature for the same period—1475–1640.

"When the Harmsworth Collection came here," Richard continued, "it made the Folger a powerhouse. For that period, we have the largest collection of printed books outside of England."

Richard was very friendly but there was something urgent in his manner, as if he wanted to reach out, grab you by the lapels, and scream, "This is a terrific place!" We found out why as soon as we left the office and headed off to the exhibition hall.

When the Folgers contracted to build this library, they had wanted to make it as authentic as possible, and when we got to the exhibition hall, we felt that we had just stepped into an English castle. The room was huge—three stories high and at least thirty yards long—with dark brown paneling on the walls, three-story windows covered by maroon curtains, and a white plaster ceiling carved with the Tudor rose. The floor was intricately tiled with the title of each of Shakespeare's thirty-seven plays set in a border. About a third of the way into the room the tragic drama mask had been inlaid, and about a third of the way past that, the comic.

But in an English castle you'd expect a certain amount of bustle. Here there was silence. Even though this was regular museum hours, and the Mall and the Library of Congress next door were teeming with visitors, we were the only four people in the room.

In an advertising brochure, they call the Folger "the best-kept secret in Washington" because, apparently, almost no tourists come here.

"We try to give Shakespeare relevance," said Richard, reading our thoughts. "We have an interactive display where a visitor can hear some of the great speeches, we allow the theater to be used not just for Shakespearean works, but for more contemporary performances as well, and we sponsor a program in which local schools can do parts of the plays here. There's a school group in there now— you'll see when we come to the theater."

Shakespeare is certainly not an easy sell. Despite the recent successes of Kenneth Branagh and Gwyneth Paltrow, Shakespeare nonetheless remains English, not American; he and his language are five hundred years old. To most people, the mention of his name and his work evokes their absolutely most unpleasant experience of high school English. The current exhibit, "Fooles and Fricassees: Food in Shakespeare's England," did not seem to be the ideal choice to overcome this prejudice. Would tourists really care how many different ways Elizabethan chefs cooked fat, butter, and cream?

Food, however, turned out to be just part of what was a unique and fascinating exhibit.

Richard began by showing us a map of England that was displayed inside a glass case. "In Shakespeare's time," he said, "maps showed more than simply the geography of a given area. Atlases told stories. They were a guide to the material world—domestic practices or how to keep immune from disease. This map was done by John Speed, a famous cartographer. As you can see, there is a good deal of information, such as modes of dress." There was a row of four figures on each side of the map, with men on the left, women on the right. "Top to bottom, here are lords, gentlemen, artisans, and commoners. Maps turn into a cultural abstract—this is one of the ways we know how people dressed in Elizabethan England."

He led us a short way down the hall and stopped at another framed display case. "There's a lot to see here, but I especially want to show you this. It's a truly one-of-a-kind book."

In the case was a single mounted page. It was labeled "August hath 31 dayes," with a verse underneath, then some information about the month, another verse, then a primitive but finely rendered illustration of a man hewing grain and a woman standing beside him with a basket on her head. We could see through the paper and on the back side there seemed to be a day-by-day listing, but we couldn't make out what it said. The detail in both the layout and the illustration was exceptional.

"This is from a pictorial commonplace book," said Richard. "A commonplace book was a combination diary, calendar, almanac, family history, and date book. There's a page for each month. This one belonged to Thomas Trevelyon and was done in 1608. This is not an artist's work—this was done by Trevelyon himself for his own family. The entire book is three hundred pages—six hundred sides. It took Trevelyon two-and-a-half years to complete the manuscript. There is only one of these in the world and it is here.

"Commonplace books recorded everything—the history of kings and queens, lace making, astronomy. These books descend from Martin Luther and the Reformation—putting knowledge in the hands of common people and getting it away from the clergy. Part of their function was to tell biblical stories to children. The illustrations generally depict some domestic or agricultural chore in keeping with the month. The books also tell how long the days and nights are, when the sun rises, and when it sets. Then, of course, there are the epigrams."

We looked carefully at the verses. The one on top read, "Dame Ceres now the empty barnes*with flore of ripened fruites doth fill*O happy naight, that grace obtaines*And strength from good, to do his will." The second verse read, "As burning heate will thee destroy*So shiverying colde will thee anoy*let lytle sleepe thee now content*purge not, nor bleed, lest thou repent."

A number of the months were displayed in various parts of the exhibit. (We noticed later that the commonplace book was a gift from—who else?—Lessing J. Rosenwald.)

"There is no better way for us to determine how people really lived during Shakespeare's time than from sources like this," said Richard.

In glass cases along the walls there were also a number of artifacts from the period, all having to do with how people ate and drank. We saw recipe books, engravings, illustrations of how to cut up a chicken, kitchen implements, broadsides, and "The women's petition against coffee"—everything relating to food or drink or barroom brawls. The recipes in particular were fascinating—no wonder nobody lived past forty.

For example, to make "a Posset without Milke," you "take 12 or 14 Eggs, beate them very well with halfe a pound of sugar." Then, after some machinations, "halfe a white-lofe" is stirred in, then "a pint of aile, and halfe a pint of Sack [sherry]." This, of course, must have been the Lo-Fat Posset—they probably left out the milk to hold down the cholesterol.

Next, Richard took us over to a small spice cabinet. It had a lock, he explained, because sugar and spices were very expensive and had to be carefully doled out.

"This item comes from an unusual collector. His name is George Way, and he's a butcher from Staten Island in New York."

At the end of the hall, in a glass case, was a large red volume opened to an illustration of Shakespeare. "This is one of our First Folios," said Richard. "Of the thirty-seven plays, about half appear here for the first time. There are no surviving texts—and only six signatures. If it weren't for this book, we would not have those plays. This is also the most reliable image we have of Shakespeare himself.

"This book was published seven years after Shakespeare died and, out of a print run of eight hundred, two hundred and forty have survived. That's a remarkable number and gives a sense of how important this book must have been considered even when it was issued. It cost almost a pound and Ben Jonson did the opening poem.

"Out of those two hundred and forty extant First Folios, we have seventy-nine. The next-largest collection is in Japan and they have eleven."

It was a beautiful book and in wonderful condition. Maybe we had been spoiled in the vault of the Library of Congress, but when it became clear that Richard had no intention of removing it from the case and showing us a page or two, we all felt an acute sense of disappointment.

The Folger has a remarkable number of programs, everything from outreach competitions for local area schools to PEN/Faulkner readings featuring such prominent authors as Diane Johnson, E. L. Doctorow, and Annie Proulx. There are also music programs and poetry seminars. The centerpiece of all of this, of course, is the collection, which, like that at the Library of Congress, is available to registered readers. The reading room at the Folger, while not on the scale of the LOC (what could be?), is nonetheless impressive. It is two stories high, ringed by handcrafted oak shelves, and at one end is a fifteen-foot-tall, magnificent stained glass window depicting the seven ages of man as described by Jaques in *As You Like It.*

At the end of our tour, we were standing on a balcony in the reading room under the window. Richard gestured across the room at the large portraits of a man and woman that hung on either side of a center partition at the other end. "Those are Henry Clay Folger and Emily Jordan Folger. Behind the partition are their ashes." He turned to us and smiled. "So you can see that the Folgers are still very much with us."

A few weeks before our trip, we had bought a copy of Herschel Parker's new Melville biography (nine hundred pages and only volume one) over the Internet from Alphaville Books in Chevy Chase, Maryland. Since we knew we were soon going to be in the neighborhood, we had asked them if there was a list of local booksellers, and they sent along *The Washington Area Booksellers Association*

(WABA), a small pamphlet that lists all member book dealers within a seventy-five-mile radius of the White House. There were more than seventy dealers—a greater number than is listed in the Connecticut Antiquarian Booksellers Guide, which covers the entire state.

Since we knew we were going to be in the Capitol district, we checked to see if there were any shops nearby. There were two: Capitol Books, which appeared to be a standard used-book store, and another, more intriguing listing:

ANTIQUES ON THE HILL—THE BOOK ANNEX
John W. Borhman III
By Appointment only, available seven days a week
Specializing: Collectable 20th Century first Editions
General Stock and Vintage Paperbacks available
Ten Blocks East of the US Capitol

We had come to learn that "by appointment only" almost always meant someone who was doing business out of his or her home. We had had very good luck with dealers like this in the past; they tended to have a smaller selection but first-rate stock, and since you're dealing with someone who doesn't have to sit in a shop all day, this kind of dealer tended to be more sociable with those who did show up. Accordingly, we had called to arrange an appointment.

"HI!" A friendly, ebullient voice had boomed out of the receiver. "IS THIS TIM?"

"Uh—no. Does it have to be?"

"OH, NO, IT'S JUST THAT I'VE BEEN DEALING WITH THIS GUY ON THE INTERNET AND HE SAID HE WAS GOING TO CALL AND I THOUGHT IT WAS GOING TO BE HIM."

"No, no. My name is Larry Goldstone. We just wanted to make an appointment to come by and see your books."

"SURE! SURE! YOU WANT TO COME BY NOW?"

"No, we're still in Connecticut. How about next Friday?"

"GREAT! WHAT TIME?"

"Well, we have an appointment at the Folger Shakespeare Library at ten, and after that we thought we'd get a little lunch—"

"OH, YOU WANT TO MEET FOR LUNCH?"

"Well, we have our daughter with us and she's eight and she only eats about four different foods, so we have to find the right kind of place—"

"OH, GO TO EASTERN MARKET. THEY HAVE ALL SORTS OF PLACES THERE."

He then proceeded to cheerfully run down a list of about five different restaurants, discussing the decor and pricing policies of each, and noting what their specialties were. This was perhaps the friendliest man on earth.

"Okay. We'll get some lunch and we'll probably be at your place about one."

"OH, NO HURRY. I'LL BE HERE. ENJOY YOUR LUNCH!"

"Well gee, thanks."

So, after the Folger and a lunch at Eastern Market, where Emily had a hot chocolate with whipped cream and scowled through three, grudging, torturous bites of a turkey-and-cucumber sandwich (light on the turkey), we made our way back to East Capitol Avenue, a clean, wide, beautiful boulevard lined with one well-tended town house after another, each one fronted by a little garden. On the north side of the street, just before Lincoln Park, we came to John Borhman's house and rang the bell.

A man opened the door. He was about fifty, wearing faded jeans and a sweatshirt. The sweatshirt had a polo emblem—not Ralph Lauren, but real polo, like with horses. He had on a polo shirt under the sweatshirt, with the collar up.

"Come on in!" he said. "I'm Jack Borhman." He stuck out his

hand and hauled us in as he shook it. He leaned down to say hi to Emily and ask her how old she was. Adults do this every time, but for some reason Emily inevitably deals with it as a trick question and pauses lengthily before replying.

Usually, when you come to see a book dealer who works out of his home, there are some brief pleasantries and then you are led immediately to where the books are—generally in a room in the basement or on the main floor, selected in such a way that you don't traipse through the person's private living quarters. Jack, however, did things a little differently.

"This is the living room," he announced, taking us into a room with wide-board floors, a high ceiling, and a big mirror propped on the mantel and leaning against the wall over the fireplace. "My wife said, 'That's the way they do it in *Architectural Digest,*'" he said. "I'm always afraid it's going to fall." There were also a number of interesting oil paintings and watercolors on the walls. "We got those in Paris . . . my wife and I go twice a year. There are some more in the kitchen, do you want to see them?"

Jack's kitchen was very nice. "We redid it," he said.

We chatted in the kitchen for a while. Jack discussed his plans for the ivy that covered an entire wall opposite the garden but told us that we couldn't go out there because the lock on the door was sticking. Then he offered us coffee, asked Emily if she wanted a soda, and talked some more about the paintings. Each of us occasionally glanced at the other, wondering if we should mention something about books, but Jack was so hospitable that it would have felt rude to hurry him.

Finally he said, "Hey. You want to see the upstairs?"

When we got to the landing on the top of the second floor, there was an office to the left. It had a desk in the middle with a computer system on it, and was ringed all around by bookshelves. As soon as we walked in, we saw that he had very good stuff.

The wall behind the desk was divided into two floor-to-ceiling sections. To the right were Jack's personal favorites—ten or fifteen writers, each of whom was extensively represented. There were Steinbeck, Jack London, Faulkner, Henry Miller, and especially D. H. Lawrence. "*Lady Chatterley's Lover* is my favorite book," he said, nodding to the ten or fifteen copies on a shelf at eye level, almost every one a different edition.

It was an impressively literary collection and not what we would have expected from a man of Jack's, uh, temperament. We asked him, as we almost always do with a dealer whom we have just met, how he had gotten started in the business.

"I used to have ten Porsches," he said. "But I traded them in for my book collection. I was racing a Formula car—not a Formula 1—in SCCA [that's Sports Car Club of America for the rest of us]. At forty-two I ran the New York City Marathon, then I played international rugby. That's the way I was . . . you know, Army officer, disabled vet, airborne Ranger. Anyway, I was driving this car and I was going too fast and I thought to myself (a) I don't want to wreck this car because I can't afford to fix it, and (b) I don't really want to wreck myself. Then a friend of ours did get killed and that was the handwriting on the wall. My wife said, 'When are you going to start reading all those books you bought?' So now I read two books a week. I mark it down on the calendar," he said.

"I made a ton of money off Ian Fleming. Luckily, he was one of the first authors I bought. I happened to have all this money coming in and I was just starting to learn about the Internet. The way it worked before was, there were these book scouts . . . they went to fairs, yard sales, everywhere . . . to look for books. Then they would go to dealers and sell them, like for twenty cents on the dollar. The dealers were marking them up to cover the costs of a Georgetown store. Then the book scouts started saying, "What am I doing this for?" and they went on the Internet and started selling the books themselves. I noticed that they were selling the books for maybe forty cents on the dollar so I bought them all up.

"The way I got into this was, I was doing mortgage banking and I met Allen Ahearn. He runs this great book store in Maryland. He had given up plans for this big house in the country and I got him all excited about it again, doing it with mortgaging. He got me excited too and I went out and bought all his reference books so I would know what I was doing.

"As soon as I was into it, I knew that the Internet was the place to be. At the time, dealers from Australia were trying to do business but nobody wanted their stuff . . . I guess it was the exchange rate or something. But I saw an Agatha Christie for forty dollars . . . it was *The Murder of Roger Ackroyd* . . . anyway we're going to Paris on what I made on that book. I sold it to a dealer for thirty-eight hundred.

"Do you use eBay?" he asked without taking a breath. "I fought doing eBay in the beginning, but if you're patient you can get some marvelous things. I only deal in authors I like, so I can narrow my searches. Also, I've learned never to buy anything that doesn't have a picture. Even so, I end up returning about half the books I buy. Either the condition isn't good, or they're book club editions . . . you have to be careful."

We checked out the shelves, where there was a row of John le Carrés. "Are all these firsts?" we asked.

"Some of them. *Call for the Dead* is a book club edition but a lot of dealers try to pass it off as a trade edition."

Call for the Dead was le Carré's first book, written when he was completely unknown. It is short, only 125 pages, and introduces a young, owlish, introspective member of the British Secret Service named George Smiley. It is a taut story, beautifully rendered and devastatingly powerful, which examines the moral conundrums and conveniently rationalized hypocrisies in a way that in a few years would make John le Carré one of the world's most widely read authors. To anyone who has been tempted to read le Carré but is put off by the seeming impenetrability of his stories, *Call for the*

Dead is the perfect introduction. A true American first, in a white dust jacket, sells for over $1,200. (We've seen the first UK priced at $13,500.) It is so uncommon that few collectors actually know what the dust jacket looks like, so the book club version, with a teal and brown dust jacket, is notorious for being passed off as a trade edition.

"What about *The Spy Who Came In from the Cold*?" we asked, pointing to another book on the shelf.

"I'm not sure about that one. It's got the three blurbs on the back of the dust jacket instead of four but it doesn't have a 'W' on the copyright page."

John le Carré, at least through *Smiley's People,* was one of those few writers who could transcend his genre and produce first-rate literature in what for most is a pop mode. *The Spy Who Came In from the Cold* is a bitter and haunting book, le Carré at his twisty, cynical best. After the runaway success of *Spy,* his third book, le Carré, who until then had been known simply as "an employee of the British Foreign Service," came out of the cold himself and was thrust into international celebrity. The first UK edition, published by Gollancz, is a plain, drab affair, selling nonetheless for close to $1,000. The first American edition, featuring a gray dust jacket and a photograph of the top of the Brandenburg Gate on the front, has quotes from Graham Greene, Alec Waugh, and Joseph Priestley on the back. The price, $4.50, is on the front inside flap. In all subsequent printings, an additional quote from Daphne du Maurier appears over the original three. We had a later printing at home, but it was one of those books for which we would have loved to trade up to a first but could never afford to do it. We had seen first Americans sell for over $300 at the New York Antiquarian Book Fair.

John's copy had a reasonably fresh dust jacket, lightly soiled with some small chips at the top of the spine but certainly comparable to most of those we had seen at fairs. On the copyright page, it did indeed read, "First American Edition," although there was, as John had said, no "W." He was selling it for $75.

"Maybe it's a book club edition," we offered and removed the dust jacket to check for the telltale debossing at the base of the back cover.

It was hard to tell. There *might* have been a little square, but it was sufficiently faint that you had to turn the book just so against the light to see a shadow. But since it seemed to lack a key issue point, the book club theory gained credibility.

"We don't know," we said. The idea of spending $75 for something that might turn out not to be a true first wasn't all that appealing. "Maybe we'll pass."

"Sure," said Jack, with a wave of his hand. "I understand. I'm not sure myself. But the dust jacket is definitely a first and I figure that it's in good enough shape to be worth seventy-five on its own."

"Definitely," we agreed.

"You know what," Jack went on, "let's check anyway."

He went around to the front of his desk and picked up a 1998 edition of *Current Book Prices*. It's a book that Allen Ahearn and his wife, Pat, produce each year, listing widely collected books with issue points and an estimate of what a fine or near-fine copy should be selling for. It is one of the bibles of the book trade.

Jack leafed through until he got to le Carré. For *The Spy Who Came In from the Cold,* it read, "First American, three quotes on rear of dust jacket, price $4.50, no 'W' on copyright page, $250."

Oops.

"Hey," said Jack happily, "I must have read it wrong. It's not supposed to have a 'W'."

"Guess not," we agreed glumly.

He turned to us. "Do you want it?"

"But it's a two-hundred-fifty-dollar book." Suddenly, the probably phantom debossing on the back cover had ceased to be an issue.

"I know. But I was selling it to you for seventy-five. If you want it, it's yours." Jack had not lost one iota of his voluble affability and there wasn't a trace of resentment in the offer.

"Well, sure, we want it . . . look, we can't buy a two-hundred-

and-fifty-dollar book from you for seventy-five because you didn't realize it was a first." Strangely enough, we meant it.

"That's okay. I'm in business to sell books and this is what I was selling this book for."

"No, really . . ."

"It's yours if you want it."

"You mean it?"

"Sure."

"Okay."

(When we got home, we checked out *The Spy Who Came In from the Cold* on the Internet. To our genuine relief, copies in roughly the same condition as ours were selling for about $125 to $150. That made it a good deal but not *so* good that we felt like pirates.)

"Oh by the way," said Jack, glancing around to make sure Emily, who had been sent off to the living room to read, hadn't wandered back upstairs, "I have some exotica I keep in the bedroom. Come on, I'll show you."

We followed Jack into his bedroom. As in the other rooms, the furnishings were somewhat sparse but the art was outstanding. There was a shelf on his side of the bed, with *Justine, Lolita,* and a few other titles. But what really stood out was a group of small oil paintings of what appeared to be street scenes of Paris.

"Yes, aren't they terrific?" Jack said. "I love those. We've got some more." He waved us toward a doorway at the far end of the room. "They're in here," he said. Then he laughed. "Don't tell my wife. She would kill me if she knew I was taking you into our bathroom."

After our visit with Jack, we went to the Supreme Court, which is not open on weekends, and, after the tour, we decided to eat in Georgetown. It was a Friday night and we figured that with all the people about, the bookstores might be open and we could save Emily a morning. So, we hiked back to the Metro by way of the carousel, bought the convenient three-ride package, then took the Blue Line four stops to Foggy Bottom (great name—one can't help but wonder as to the derivation). There is no Metro station in Georgetown proper, so it was another pretty good hike to get there.

All the bookstores were closed. Booked Up, the shop that is co-owned by Larry McMurtry and that we had been particularly interested in seeing, had a chain across the staircase. The actual entrance was One Flight Up, so we couldn't even read what the Saturday hours were, although we assumed they'd be open at least from eleven to five. Emily was exhausted. Every restaurant seemed to be either Mexican, Vietnamese, Indian, or Burmese. Despite our warnings that this was a new food trip, it didn't seem fair to make her go from spaghetti in tomato sauce to burritos, so we found yet another unspeakable Italian restaurant, where the waiter, after we had ordered our chiantis, suggested, "What about a cranberry juice for the young lady?" then charged us four dollars for it.

At about nine-thirty, we straggled back to the hotel. The advantage of staying at Embassy Suites is that each room is, in fact, a suite, so that parents can have that extra teeny bit of privacy while their offspring sleep in what is at least titularly another room. Emily was too tired for a bath, so she just sort of fell into bed, while we retired to the grown-up section.

After a moment or two, we heard a plaintive voice coming from the other room.

"Where's Bearite?"

Bearite, you will remember, was the little white bear with enormous sentimental value.

"What do you mean, sweetie? Isn't he on the bed somewhere with the other animals?"

"No."

A search ensued. Each of us has written unsuccessful detective novels, so we know how to toss a room. After ten minutes of looking in places where only the most sophisticated drug dealer would hide a stash (in the curtain well, under the flap of the swivel chair, in the crack between the television and the cabinet), it became sickeningly apparent that Bearite was no longer with us.

When the truth finally hit, Emily at first tried to tough it out. It probably took fifteen or twenty seconds before the tears actually began to roll down her cheeks. The problem was that Bearite was just a baby—he couldn't even talk yet. That Bearite had been a baby who couldn't even talk yet for the four years Emily had owned him didn't matter at all. "He'll be scared," Emily said between sobs. "He's so little."

The first order of business, we knew, was to make it through the night.

"Oh Emily," said one of us with blatantly forced good cheer. "That ol' Bearite. He's probably just hiding. I'll bet he jumped into the maid's cart. He'll be back in the morning."

Emily wanted to believe this, although the skepticism in her eyes was intense.

"Sure," we went on, "just wait and see."

One of us padded off to the telephone and called the front desk. "My daughter's stuffed bear is missing it must have gotten mixed up in the sheets we need someone to go down to the laundry RIGHT AWAY or our trip will be ruined."

But the laundry was closed, not to reopen until 9:30 in the morning. We were assured however that a sheet-by-sheet search would be instituted until Bearite was recovered.

The disappearance of Bearite, however, meant that we all not only slept in the same room, we slept in the same bed.

Early the next morning, before Emily woke up, one of us snuck down to the front desk. A helpful but funereal assistant manager had heard all about Bearite.

"I went and looked in the laundry myself," he said. "I didn't find a stuffed bear. All I can think of is that maybe it got thrown into the washing machine. We have commercial machines—they're very powerful. They might have chewed the bear up completely and the laundry staff wouldn't have known what the leftover fuzz was."

Bearite ripped to shreds in a washing machine? No way we were going to relate *that* story to Emily. (It also makes you wonder about what the sheets must be made of.)

Next to where the assistant manager was standing was a placard that read:

100% GUARANTEE
We guarantee high quality accommodations,
friendly and efficient service,
and clean and comfortable surroundings.
If you are not completely satisfied, we don't expect you to pay.

The assistant manager glanced toward it, and then said immediately, "Of course, we'll take the first night off the bill."

That was not exactly what the guarantee said, but it seemed to be Embassy Suites' standard opening offer. Just before the Bearite discussion, a man who had complained that his room had been about 130 degrees all night had received the same rebate. Still, the first night, a higher rate since it was a weekday, came to about $240, including tax, and so as not to appear greedy, the offer was accepted.

Well, one of us thought with unforgivable cynicism, at least Bearite died in a good cause. We ate breakfast (free—Embassy Suites is actually a terrific deal) then got out of there as quickly as we could. We weren't sure how much diversion going to bookstores in Georgetown would provide, but we knew that the less time spent at the scene of the tragedy, the better. What's more, *we'd* started to miss Bearite.

We got to Georgetown at about eleven. As we walked from the Metro, the first of the five shops we came to was Bartleby's, which was on the second floor of a two-story building on the corner of M and 30th Streets, NW. Bartleby's was right over a hair salon and the smell of permanent solution was overpowering and made us all a little light-headed as we climbed up the narrow stairs.

Bartleby's was one large room with a golden narrow-planked wooden floor, white walls, and track lighting spotlighting the books. At one end were gothic floor-to-ceiling windows that let in light from the street. The walls were lined with shelves and there were three freestanding bookshelves, including a glass-fronted one, placed diagonally toward the front. The back of the shop, where there were more rows of bookshelves, was separated from the front by a long counter. Under the counter were glass display cases. You can't always judge by interior design, of course, but this kind of tastefulness usually means that the books are going to be good. Expensive maybe, but good.

We started with the bookshelves along the front wall. These were solid, used books, not particularly expensive and certainly a superior selection—Elizabeth Bowen, John Cheever, Theodore Dreiser, essays on John Dryden, E. M. Forster. Whoever had organized the shelves had done it with an eye toward the whole literary experience—each author's section contained biographical information, criticism, and letters along with the fiction.

But it was the freestanding glass-fronted bookcases in the front that contained the real gems. These were indeed more expensive but by no means overpriced. There were all sorts of neat titles, like *A Trojan Ending* by Laura Riding and *this ROOM & this GIN & these SANDWICHES* by Edmund Wilson, which featured a dust jacket with a great pen-and-ink drawing of a table with a half-eaten sandwich, a leaning bottle of gin, and a still-smoking cigarette dangling over the end. There were also *Eggs, Beans and Crumpets* by P. G. Wodehouse and—startlingly—*The Works of Max Beerbohm*.

The Works of Max Beerbohm was published when the author was twenty-two; it was a collection of all of Beerbohm's writings to that date—all seven essays to be precise. The book was a small, unprepossessing red leather volume, with uncut pages and a simple title band across the spine. It was a first edition, one of a thousand copies, printed in 1896 by The Bodley Head in London. It contained a bibliography by John Lane and was in remarkably good condition. There was no foxing on the pages (those unsightly brown spots), the spine was unbroken, and the paper had retained its crispness. It was $150.

As it happened, we'd seen this book before. Not for sale, but at the Beinecke Library at Yale, which was the only place we had found in Connecticut that had a copy. But the Beinecke copy had been *terrible*—foxed and falling apart. Given how few copies seemed to be around and that this was *Yale,* we had simply assumed that all the copies were in similar disrepair. Here, however, for a mere $150 was a far superior copy for less than it would cost to own *Cold Mountain.* Plus, we'd have a better copy than the Beinecke and there'd be no forms to fill out.

"Larr-rr-rr-y—"

"Yeah, yeah, yeah. Why is it that all the books I want cost sixteen dollars and all the books you want cost two hundred?"

"I have better taste."

"Are you really going to read it?"

"How can you ask such a thing?"

"It's not just going to sit on the bookshelf and look rare?"

"Of course not." There was a conspiratorial glance toward the front of the store, where Emily was reading, followed by a barely audible whisper. "There *is* the Bearite money."

The Works was brought to the counter.

While we were hanging around waiting to squander Bearite's legacy, we checked out the display cases in front of the cash register. There was some great Americana:

- *Life of the Siamese Twins* for $450.
- Joseph B. Cobb: *Mississippi Scenes; or, Sketches of Southern and Western Life and Adventure, Humorous, Satirical, and Descriptive, Including the Legend of Black Creek* (Phil. A. Hart, 1851).

- Lionel Chalmers, MD, of Charles-Town: *An Account of Weather and Diseases of South Carolina* (London, E&C Dilly, 1776, two volumes, $4,500).

As we were marching down the stairs, the ill-gotten Beerbohm in a plain brown wrapper, we both looked at Emily.

"You can have spaghetti for lunch, sweetie," we said graciously.

Our next stop, after lunch, was Booked Up. When we got there, the chain on the staircase was off, but when we went up the steps, we found that the store was once again closed. A sign on the door read, "Open Saturdays 10–12:30," and it was now a quarter to one. We peeked in the window—it certainly looked like a good store. It must have been, because here it was, a beautiful fall weekend with the streets packed with young men and women walking around with discretionary income practically falling out of their pockets, and Booked Up did not feel any need whatever to stay open.

And so we went a couple of doors down the street to The Antiquarian Book Shop, which is owned by William Hale, who, according to the literature, is a distant relative of Nathan Hale.

The shop was small, a single narrow room that appeared to be not more than about eight hundred square feet. It was ringed by floor-to-ceiling bookshelves, with a table stacked with books in the middle. Sticking out prominently was a perfectly disreputable, oversized book with a cheap cover and almost no spine, which Emily made for like a shot.

"Look," she said excitedly. "*The Big Book of Dogs!*"

It was indeed. On the cover was an artist's conception of a large, bemused hound of indeterminate origin with two perky little Scotties underneath. It was $15.

"Maybe there's a beagle in it!" said Emily.

We handed Emily the book to look at, having already, in this post-Bearite period, kissed the $15 good-bye. As she retired to a small stool in the corner, we had a look at some of the other books on the table. *The Big Book of Dogs* was not the only selection with a canine theme. There was:

The Werewolf by Montague Summers, subtitled *The Werewolf: Lycanthropy; The Werewolf: His Science and Practice; The Werewolf in Greece and Italy, Spain and Portugal; The Werewolf in England and Wales, Scotland and Ireland; The Werewolf in the North, in Russia and Germany; The Werewolf in France/Witch Ointments,* which seemed to be a lot of werewolves for $25.

There was also *Rowan Tree & Red Thread: A Scottish Witchcraft Miscellany—Tales, Legends and Ballads together with a Description of the Witches' Rites and Ceremonies* by Thomas Davidson for $40.

"Those come from the collection of a professor of folklore who specialized in the werewolf in literature. Now he's writing a novel. It's a scholar's collection of esoterica," volunteered a woman sitting behind a small desk toward the back. She was youngish looking, with long brown hair pulled back off her face and held by a barrette.

"My name is Candy Harris," she said, and told us that she had been working with Bill Hale for the past fifteen years. "Bill's been here for twenty-two years," Candy went on. "I started when some friends decided to open a bookstore. I happened to have the three thousand dollars they needed to start up with and within six months I was full-time with books. Eventually, I ended up here."

We walked over to one of the bookcases against the wall. A lot of the titles were foreign. For example, there was:

Nederlands Displegtigheden [Netherlands Described]
Poor
K. Van Alkemade
en
Mr. Van Der Schelling
Rotterdam, by Philippus Losel, 1732.

It was in the original Dutch in three volumes with fold-out engravings for $850.

"Bill does the European auctions," Candy said. "That's mostly about drinking. It's culinary. Drinking and drinking cups.

"In this store, we work on the principle of buying things we don't see very much," she added.

That certainly seemed true. Where else might you find *Self Propelled Vehicles: A Practical Illustrated Treatise on Automobiles* by J. E. Homans, seventh edition, 1910, revised?

"Most mechanical guides are falling apart, they've got grease all over them," Candy pointed out. "This one's clean."

We chatted some more. When we were ready to leave, Emily walked over and looked up at us, *The Big Book of Dogs* held tightly under her arm.

"Why don't you take that?" Candy said to her. "No charge."

Our next stop was The Old Forest Bookshop, around the corner and down the street. Old Forest was housed in a neat red brick two-story town house with a green awning, matching green door, and old-fashioned sign. It had an excellent literary biography section upstairs and a well-stocked cookbook section on the main floor. There were old record albums and paperback mysteries in addition to a general stock of used books in good condition. There was even a nook for children's books.

We found a nice volume of Kay Boyle short stories for ten dollars, then quit. If we had gone to Old Forest first, we might have spent a lot more time browsing. But, as so often happens, by the time we got to the last shop on our list, we were a little booked out (as opposed to Booked Up), so we gathered up our purchases and ran the gauntlet of the ice-cream shops on M Street.

We'll spare you a description of the rest of our trip except to say that when we went to Ford's Theater, the man who gave the talk was phenomenal—he was so excited and so animated that when he made the sound of gunshots, everyone in the audience jumped. (He's a heavyish man of about fifty. If you're planning on going, don't settle for anyone else.)

Sunday night we could put it off no longer and broke the news to Emily that Bearite wasn't coming back. Suffice to say that it was a long night with lots of tears—not all of them Emily's. By the time we got to the airport the next day, she was soldiering her way through, but we could see that she was genuinely distraught. The plane was delayed, so we asked her, "Would you like to try and find another animal? Not to replace Bearite, but someone else to love?"

After a very brief search, we found White-ite. Like his unfortunate predecessor, White-ite was also a white bear. He was bigger, cleaner, very fluffy, and on sale for $4.99. Emily hugged White-ite the whole way home.

The very next day, the telephone rang.

"Mr. Goldstone?"

"Yes?"

"This is the Embassy Suites in Alexandria. You're not going to believe this, but when we were looking in the laundry chute, we found your daughter's bear. It must have been stuck there all weekend. It's in perfect shape. I'm sure your daughter will be relieved. If it's all right, we'll overnight it to you."

"Thank you! That's wonderful!"

"I'm sure we had looked in the chute before—I don't know how we could have missed it."

After we hung up the phone, we walked into our library and checked out our new copy of *The Works of Max Beerbohm.*

That ol' Bearite.

Chapter 2

THE INCOMPARABLE MAX

Just before 2 P.M. on the afternoon of June 3, 1997, a number of unusual visitors began to drift furtively into the venerable Round Reading Room of the British Museum. They came in all shapes and sizes and were of varying nationalities. A couple of them wore strange costumes. Some were celebrities. A former chief inspector of prisons was there, as was a scion of an ancient aristocratic British family. The rest included a noted English actor, a famed antiquarian book dealer, and an American magician. None had the special reader's card that is ordinarily required for admission.

The library regulars gazed at the strangers with a mixture of curiosity and irritation. "Who are all these people?" said one. "They should be washed out of here with a water cannon."

The visitors, unfazed, milled about. Each had arrived for a clandestine appointment at precisely 2:10 P.M., and as the moment approached, "[They] waited with expectation bordering on fanaticism," according to that most trusted and reliable of newspapers, the *London Daily Telegraph*. Each was there to meet a man they knew only by a description that had appeared in a book:

He was a stooping, shambling person, rather tall, very pale, with longish and brownish hair. He had a thin vague beard—or rather, he had a chin on which a large number of hairs weakly curled and clustered to cover its retreat. . . . He wore a soft black hat of the clerical kind but of Bohemian intention, and a grey waterproof cape which, perhaps because it was waterproof, failed to be romantic.

His name was Enoch Soames.

Enoch Soames was a poet. He was not a very good poet—in fact, his poetry was dreadful. His major published work, *Fungoids,* had sold only three copies. These lines are from his most famous poem, "To A Young Woman":

> *Thou art, who hast not been!*
> Pale tunes irresolute
> And traceries of old sounds
> Blown from a rotted flute
> Mingle with noise of cymbals rouged with rust,
> Nor not strange forms and epicene
> Lie bleeding in the dust,
> Being wounded with wounds.

What made Enoch Soames notable was obviously not lines like these, but the circumstances of his short life. For Enoch Soames had disappeared exactly one hundred years before. His last sighting had been at a down-at-the-heels Soho café in 1897.

It happened like this: Soames, convinced that he was a poet before his time (instead of the poet of no time that the fin de siècle literary community considered him), had made a pact with the devil—he would agree to eternal damnation for the right to return to earth exactly one century later and see the huge volume of work not only by him, but about him as well. Soames had made this pact at 2:10 P.M. on June 3, 1897, and then abruptly vanished into the future. The location that Soames had chosen to confirm his place in history was the Round Reading Room of the British Museum.

Later in the afternoon of that same day in 1897, Soames reappeared briefly. He sat miserably at the same café, drinking. According to a reliable observer, Soames's despair was caused, not by the prospect of eternal damnation, but by what he had found during his trip to the future. Instead of reams of citations, there had been only one reference to "Soames, Enoch," and that was a casual mention in a volume on late nineteenth-century literature by a Mr. T. K. Nupton. Mr. Nupton wrote using phonetic spelling, but translated the passage read:

> For example, a writer of the time, named Max Beerbohm, who was still alive in the twentieth century, wrote a story in which he portrayed an imaginary character called "Enoch Soames"—a third-rate poet who believed himself a great genius and made a bargain with the Devil in order to know what posterity thought of him! It is a somewhat labored satire but not without value as showing how seriously the young men of the eighteen-nineties took themselves. . . .

This paragraph was, of course, written by Max Beerbohm himself and appeared in his classic short story, "Enoch Soames."

The first time we encountered the name Max Beerbohm was in a catalog from Swann's auction house. They were offering a first edition of something called *Zuleika Dobson,* written in 1912, for which the estimated selling price was $200–$250.

For some reason, this book attracted our interest. Without ever having read a word he had written, solely on the basis of the sound of his name, we somehow leapt to the conclusion that Max Beerbohm was a German anarchist, the kind of person who hung around with Emma Goldman. *Zuleika Dobson,* therefore, must be an earnest, important book about the plight of the working class, most likely the story of a poor immigrant girl growing up in the shadow of a steel mill or coal mine in Chicago or Cleveland or Stuttgart or somewhere.

It sounded worthwhile, but $250 was a lot of money to pay for an Upton Sinclair knockoff. You never know what will happen at an auction, however, so we decided that if there was no interest, we might consider taking a flyer. Unfortunately, *Zuleika Dobson* actually exceeded its high estimate, and we ended up buying *Goodbye, Mr. Chips* for $80 instead.

So sure had we been that Max Beerbohm was a subversive political philosopher that we actually used his name in a book proposal we floated a couple of years ago called *"So You Think You Want to Move to the Country: Our Seven Years in the Berkshires,"* although by this time, for no reason whatever, we had reversed Max's assumed political convictions and made him a reactionary.

It was early May and we were spending a weekend with Howard and Becky, friends of ours who owned a second home in the Berkshires. Howard was in his thirties, almost six feet tall but thickly built, like a "D" battery, so that he looked shorter. He had gone to Dartmouth and took great pride in his conversion from Jewish–New Deal–liberal to Jewish neoconservative intellectual. He subscribed to the *National Review,* was an almost fanatical defender of Judge Bork, and read and quoted people like Claude Levi-Strauss and **Max Beerbohm.** In a place with one of the lowest crime rates in the northeast, Howard could not be shaken in his conviction that violent felons were lurking just around the hedgerows and had installed a state-of-the-art alarm system, complete with electric eyes and motion sensors. He was convinced that a worldwide depression was both inevitable and imminent. In order to be prepared, he hoarded canned goods in the basement. Howard knew, on an intellectual level, that life was supposed to be fun, so he told jokes, played charades, and conducted touch football games on the front lawn, but did so with the forced ebullience of a man who has just been told that he has six months to live.

Not surprisingly, that book proposal did not result in an advance.

About a year later, we were browsing in John Sanderson's basement in Stockbridge, Massachusetts, when, on the top shelf, we saw *Zuleika Dobson* once more. We took it down to have a look.

The first hint we got that we might have been a tad off the mark about old Max was when we opened to the title page and noticed that the full title, rather than the expected *Zuleika Dobson: Humiliated and Abused,* was actually *Zuleika Dobson: An Oxford Romance.* We asked John if he knew anything about the book and the author.

"Oh, sure," he replied. "Max Beerbohm was a noted wit and dandy. He's extremely well known. That's a very nice copy. It's only two hundred dollars."

Two hundred dollars was still a lot to spend, even if it was to atone for a mistake, so we returned *Zuleika Dobson* to the shelf once more.

We had forgotten all about Max until, several years later, the Modern Library published its now-notorious list of the one hundred best novels of the twentieth century. And son of a gun, there it was, number fifty-nine, wedged in between Edith Wharton's *Age of Innocence* and Walker Percy's *The Moviegoer*—*Zuleika Dobson* by Max Beerbohm.

As it happened, we were in the Hamptons visiting Aunt Cecile soon after the list came out. Aunt Cecile is a painter. She is about five-foot-two in her mules, wears prominent designer costume jewelry, and is given to long theatrical stories, in which the listener is often referred to as "darling." Her paintings are large, geometric landscapes, cityscapes, and interiors, with bold and striking colors. Her taste is unusual, sophisticated, and eclectic—she can put leopard skins with lemon yellow and make it work. She is exceedingly well read and her circle of acquaintances includes many prominent writers and musicians. Her house is littered with presentation copies inscribed by people like James Jones, Irwin Shaw, and Peter Matthiessen, which would ordinarily be terrific except that all her copies are completely beat-up and usually lacking dust jackets because Aunt Cecile has the odd notion that books are meant to be read.

Aunt Cecile was married to Uncle Buddy, the composer Irwin Bazelon, who had died two years before. Uncle Buddy's symphonies and other compositions have been played at Lincoln Center and Tanglewood and by prestigious orchestras abroad. He was particularly fond of percussion. "I am always looking for the space between the notes," he once said when asked about his philosophy of music.

Uncle Buddy and Aunt Cecile lived in a sprawling, four-bedroom, three-bath, prewar apartment on Lexington Avenue in Manhattan. They had bought their little place in the Hamptons with a serendipitous inheritance from Great-Aunt Ethabelle, who was herself famous for having been the longtime "private secretary" of William Hale Thompson, "Big Bill," the mayor of Chicago during the Capone era. After Big Bill died, Ethabelle sued to get a Big Chunk of the estate as compensation for all the time and effort she had put into Big Bill. She lost, but the suit prompted a famous Chicago political cartoon during the war, which was captioned "Millions for defense, not a penny for Ethabelle." Ethabelle got the last laugh, however, since she went on to marry the man who owned the exclusive rights to distribute Sony products in the United States.

But to get back to *Zuleika Dobson,* after Uncle Buddy died, Aunt Cecile continued to go to the house in the Hamptons every summer, but she needed company, so we'd bring Emily and visit for a few days. Emily adores Aunt Cecile. There were only two bedrooms, so we shared one and Emily and Aunt Cecile had the other. The two of them were like sorority sisters. Every morning around eight, we heard them moving around in the other bedroom. Aunt Cecile would take out a piece of jewelry and say things like, "Now *this* is by Perreti, darling," and Emily would sigh and say, "Oh, that's *so* pretty. May I try it on?"

One morning over breakfast, we had a discussion of the Modern Library fiction list with Aunt Cecile in which, among other things, she said that she had never read *Zuleika Dobson* either. That afternoon, we left Emily and drove to Sag Harbor to visit Canio's, one of the local used-book stores. Actually, Canio's was a bit of a hybrid. In the case in the front were new books, heavy on serious fiction and the latest offering by the Hamptons' enormous contingent of well-known authors, as well as literary magazines like *Granta* and the *Paris Review.* (They also have a small gallery for local artists and feature poetry readings on Saturday nights.) Other than that, however, Canio's was an authentic old-fashioned used-book store, the kind we love. Every inch of wall space, including the tiny alcoves in the back, was covered with knocked-together pine board floor-to-ceiling bookcases, each of which was crammed with used books. On the floor in front of almost all of the cases were piles of books obscuring the lower shelves. In addition, there were freestanding bookcases wherever space permitted and in some cases where it didn't.

As soon as we walked into the front room, we made our way to the woman behind the desk.

"Have you got a copy of *Zuleika Dobson*?" we asked.

"No."

"Have you got anything at all by Max Beerbohm?"

"Well, not *by* Max Beerbohm, but there's this," she said, getting up and pulling out a volume from one of the shelves.

"This" was *Portrait of Max: An Intimate Memoir of Sir Max Beer-*

bohm, written by S. N. Behrman. It was a 1960 book club edition. The beat-up dust jacket featured a caricature of an older man smoking a cigarette. The man had a huge, mostly bald head with little white wisps of hair at the sides over the ears, large childlike eyes, and a body tapering to a point, like a genie coming out of a bottle. It was $7.50 and we took it.

Never has an author endeared himself to us as promptly and as thoroughly as did Max Beerbohm. Early in Behrman's book, he describes his first meeting with the man. It was in 1952, when Max was eighty years old, living in a hospice in Italy with the fifty-something Miss Jungmann, who would later become his second wife in a deathbed ceremony.

Behrman was nervous. Not only was he meeting a living legend (it was Sir Max by that time), but Miss Jungmann had also warned him that Max did not like to be the one doing all the talking.

Remembering Miss Jungmann's briefing, I jumped in. Before I left New York, having found Max's books unobtainable except in libraries, I had discussed with a friend the possibility of getting all of Max's works together in a Modern Library Giant. I now told Max about this project. I explained to him that there were Giant Faulkners, Giant Hemingways, and so on.

"How would you like to be a Giant, Sir Max?" I asked.

"I should have to get an entirely new wardrobe," he said regretfully, with the air of a man who already has all the clothes he wants. "Many people have tried to make a success of me," he added, by way of apology for having doused a well-meant effort. "Would you like to see a publisher's statement?" he asked, and turned to Miss Jungmann. "Elisabeth! Do get that publisher's statement that came from Knopf."

Miss Jungmann rose and left the table.

"Mr. Knopf has had the intrepidity to reissue a book of my essays called *Yet Again*," Max said. . . . Miss Jungmann returned with the publisher's statement. Obviously, Max couldn't wait to show it to me. "*There's* a publisher's statement," he caroled as he handed it to me. His soft but penetrating voice conveyed the jubilance of an author whose book has just been accepted by the Book-of-the-Month Club. Prepared for astronomical figures, I stared at the statement. On the right-hand side was an unbroken column of zeroes. "Not one copy!" crowed Max in triumph. "NOT ONE!"

You gotta love the guy.

Max Beerbohm defies classification. He was a man-about-town who frequented music halls and actresses, but who nonetheless lived with his mother, occupying his childhood bedroom, until his late thirties. An influential theater critic who didn't much care for the theater, an artist who cheerfully skewered his friends in caricatures so wicked that a police inspector hung the one of Oscar Wilde in his office as evidence, a novelist and essayist for whom the act of writing was apparently a form of exquisite torture—Max was all of these. The toast of English society, a man who dined out every night for years and years, he ended up by marrying Florence Kahn, an actress and Tennessee Jewess, and retiring with her to an obscure villa in Italy, where the couple lived reclusively for some fifty years. For this extraordinary move, Max gave the following explanation:

"'How many people are there in London?' asked Max.

'About five million,' said the other.

'I knew them all!' said Max."*

---

*Quotations are from *Max, a Biography* by David Cecil (first American edition, Houghton Mifflin Company: Boston, 1965).

And he had. He lived a life that was at once perfectly sheltered and perfectly public. He was on an amiably social footing with, among others, Aubrey Beardsley, George Bernard Shaw, Oscar Wilde (and Alfred Douglas), Reginald Turner, Virginia Woolf, Arthur Symons, Richard Le Gallienne, Thomas Hardy, Rudyard Kipling (although they loathed each other), Algernon Swinburne, George Moore, W. B. Yeats, William Nicholson, Edmund Gosse, James McNeill Whistler, Andrew Land, and Henry James. "I am what the writers of obituary notices call 'an interesting link with the past,' " observed Max in a 1936 BBC radio broadcast entitled "A Small Boy Seeing Giants."

Max was born in 1872 in Kensington. His father, Julius Ewald Beerbohm, emigrated to England from Memel on the Baltic Sea in order to become a naturalized English citizen and corn merchant. Julius's first wife, Constantia Draper, died at thirty-two, leaving four children, one of whom, Herbert, was later to achieve some substantial notoriety of his own.

Undaunted by his first wife's death, and apparently harboring an unbiased attachment to the Draper women, Julius proceeded to marry Constantia's sister, Eliza. This was a little awkward, as there existed in England at the time a law expressly prohibiting a person from marrying his dead wife's sister. Julius, a man of some enterprise, circumvented this rule by marrying Eliza in Switzerland, and afterwards returning to London a respectable married man, since there was apparently no restriction on a person who had *already* married his dead wife's sister someplace else. Max was one of three children born to this second Mrs. Julius Beerbohm.

Max was much influenced growing up by two of his older half brothers—Julius, a romantic but impecunious adventurer, and Herbert, who appended "Tree" to his last name and went on to become one of Britain's most celebrated stage performers. (There was a third half brother, Ernest, but he immigrated to Cape Colony and became a sheep farmer. There is no evidence that either South Africa or sheep had any subsequent influence on Max's work.)

"I asked Max where Herbert got the name Tree," S. N. Behrman wrote.

> "Well," said Max, "when he first went on the stage, he had the fantasy, which became actual, that he would one day be a star. I don't suppose he could imagine the gallery, after a triumphant performance, shouting with enthusiasm for 'Beerbohm, Beerbohm!' He had the prescience, don't you know, to supply a shoutable monosyllable."

Max drew a caricature of his stepbrother once. Herbert is depicted standing with his back arched, hips and chest thrust forward, head held haughtily at profile, mouth almost scowling, large nose raised, one eye staring ferociously into the distance. He's wearing a black silk top hat and frock coat and his face, hat, and cravat are colored in, while the rest of him is in outline. He's very tall, judging from the length of the cane that Max has him leaning against—just a long thin line. His torso balloons out over absurdly gracefully poised legs and delicately pointed shoes. He looks like an immense trout posing as a maitre d'.

Max went to Oxford, where he had Lord Randolph Churchill's old room. He did no work but was immensely popular, possibly because on school holidays he could take *his* chums over to London to see Herbert's show at Herbert's theater (and at Herbert's expense). Afterwards, they would all dine in private rooms with Herbert's company and Herbert's famous friends—it was in this way that Max met Oscar Wilde. Max left Oxford after two years—he wasn't going to pass anyway—having already made a name for himself in London with the publication of a very slight essay in the *Yellow Book,* a journal put together by a group of artists and writers led by Aubrey Beardsley who collectively went by the name "the Decadents." Max's essay, a piece of frippery entitled "A Defense of Cosmetics," in which he propounded the theory that ladies who rouged were more attractive than those who didn't, caused a great deal of indignation in the legitimate press, which took it seriously as a kind of Victorian "heroin-chic" piece.

The resulting publicity made Max. He lived on it until 1898 when, in another piece of astoundingly good luck, George Bernard Shaw abruptly quit his post as dramatic critic for the prestigious *Saturday Review* and tapped the twenty-six-year-old Max as his successor. "The younger generation is knocking at the door," Shaw wrote in his last review, "and as I open it there steps sprightly in the incomparable Max."

Max was known as much for bon mots and elaborate practical jokes as for his prose. "They were a tense and peculiar family, the Oedipuses, weren't they?" he once wrote to a friend. His knighthood was held up for twenty years because, at the time of King George V's death, although publicly solemn, privately Max penned a little sonnet about a lady-in-waiting to the Queen and one of the King's manservants having an argument. The lady-in-waiting claims that the Queen is duller than the King. The manservant insists that it is the King who is duller. The argument escalates until the manservant kills first the lady-in-waiting and then himself, dying with this mantra on his lips: "The King—is—duller than the—Queen." The poem fell into the hands of the Royal Family. "Kind friends sent it to them," explained Max.

Max's chief talent, however, was not in language at all—it was in art. He was the premier caricaturist of his day, or perhaps any day. He combined the caricaturist's touch of choosing just the right physical trait for exaggeration with a legendary wit, thus enabling him to capture not only a person's physical eccentricities but his or her inner foibles as well. For example, he once depicted the poet Samuel Taylor Coleridge sitting at the head of a dining room table, surrounded by male guests. Coleridge is shown in profile so that half of the guests have their backs to the viewer, while the others, across the table, can be observed full face. It is clearly late, dinner is done, and all that is left on the table are little cordial glasses. The guests with their backs to the viewer all have their heads facedown on the table; the ones across from them are all leaning back against one another, mouths agape, snoring loudly, deeply and voluptuously asleep. Coleridge alone is awake and gesturing. "Samuel Taylor Coleridge, table-talking," reads the caption.

There are various books of Max's caricatures—he drew over two thousand of them, not counting private doodles for friends and family—but an excellent representative sample can be found in N. John Hall's *Max Beerbohm Caricatures,* which was published in 1997 by Yale University Press. Hall provides not only copies of the drawings, but also amusing introductions to and anecdotes about the personalities depicted. This is quite useful since many of Max's subjects, while famous in his day, have long since faded from public consciousness. Max drew everybody from Winston Churchill to Mark Twain but many of us need help when it comes to identifying people like Lord Burnham and Mr. Hugh Hammersley.

The beauty of collecting Max is that he is still largely affordable. Even his original caricatures are not expensive, as art goes, which is why we don't collect art. The most famous book of caricatures published in Max's lifetime was *Rossetti and His Circle,* a book of drawings of people like Aubrey Beardsley, Algernon Swinburne, William Morris, and Edward Burne-Jones, in addition to Rossetti himself. It was published in 1922 by Heinemann, with twenty-three of Max's drawings on stiff paper tipped in, and a brief introduction by the man himself. The book came out with a dust jacket of plain brown paper, almost exactly like brown wrapping paper. Many of the original purchasers probably threw the paper away, so copies in the dust jacket are reasonably rare. Still, two years ago at the New York Antiquarian Book Fair, we got an excellent copy in an almost perfect dust jacket for $175, which is pretty cheap by New York Antiquarian Book Fair standards. Having the tipped-in caricatures—they look like little postcards—is like having miniatures of the originals. The one that makes us laugh the most shows Oscar Wilde holding a long-stemmed orchid, dressed in knee-britches, stockings, and patent-leather pumps, and standing on a stage with a row of bearded, glowering, somberly dressed men in obviously cheap, ill-fitting suits sitting behind him and an audience of the same in front of him. On the wall are a pair of crossed American flags and a picture of a long-necked, scowling Abraham Lincoln. The caption reads:

THE NAME OF DANTE GABRIEL ROSSETTI IS HEARD FOR THE FIRST TIME IN THE UNITED STATES OF AMERICA. TIME: 1881. LECTURER: MR. OSCAR WILDE.

Max produced essays, short stories, and two novels as well. To be absolutely honest, *Zuleika Dobson* is by no means Max's best work. (We get the feeling the Modern Library judges knew this but were loath to leave someone of Sir Max's talents off the list, so they stuck the novel on there the way the Academy of Motion Picture Arts and Sciences puts out a Lifetime Achievement Award.) *Zuleika Dobson* is a satire about a beautiful but extremely vain young woman who arrives at Oxford for a visit and causes the entire student body to commit suicide by throwing themselves into the river for love of her. (She's upset for an hour or two, then hires a special train to take her to Cambridge.)

Certainly, *Zuleika Dobson* contains some hilarious passages, such as when the hero, a young duke attending Oxford as an undergraduate, proposes: "I, John, Albert, Edward, Claude, Orde, Angus, Tankerton, Tanville-Tankerton, fourteenth Duke of Dorset, Marquis of Dorset, Earl of Grove, Earl of Chastermaine, Viscount Brewsby, Baron Grove, Baron Petstrap, and Baron Wolock, in the Peerage of England, offer you my hand." Still, it's a one-joke novel that never approaches the depth and perspicacity of Max's other work.

It is in his essays and short stories, rather than in the novels, that Max displays something approaching the real wit and bite of the caricatures. Max's stories, of which "Enoch Soames" is the acknowledged masterpiece, are brilliant little gems skewering British society during the Victorian and Edwardian eras. One of our other favorites is "Hilary Maltby and Stephen Braxton," which is about two competing authors who cannot seem to get away from one another. Both published highly successful first novels whose titles were suspiciously similar (Maltby's was *Ariel in Mayfair* and Braxton's *A Faun on the Cotswolds*). Both followed these with conspicuous flops. Both had their names in the newspapers, both were seen at fashionable literary teas: "Indeed, it seemed impossible for either author to outvie the other in success and glory. Week in, week out, you saw cancelled either's every momentary advantage. A neck-and neck race," wrote Max.

Finally, while Maltby is attending the Annual Soiree of the Inkwomen's Club, the duchess of Hertfordshire asks if he would like to attend a small weekend gathering at her country estate. This is a big coup. He accepts, and almost immediately the duchess asks the inevitable question—did Mr. Maltby think that Mr. Braxton would like to come as well? Mr. Maltby, seeing his opportunity, dissuades the duchess from asking Braxton (who is, of course, also attending the Annual Soiree). Gloating, Maltby attends the duchess's gathering—only to be haunted the entire time by Braxton's ghost. So profoundly is he spooked (pun intended) by this affair that he throws off his entire literary career and retires to a small seaside inn.

All of Max's short stories are contained in two volumes, one entitled *Seven Men,* the other *A Christmas Garland.* We got a first American edition of *Seven Men,* one of two thousand copies printed. The book was not in peak condition, but it contained an appendix and six drawings not published elsewhere. Best of all, it was ten dollars.

After a while, we decided that it might be interesting to try to talk with someone who actually knew something about Max. A collector, perhaps. Not a dilettante, schlemiel collector, like us, but a REAL collector. The kind of collector that most dealers say hardly exists anymore. We made a few phone calls. Did anyone know anyone who collected Max Beerbohm?

"You want Mark Samuels Lasner," said a high-end New York dealer.

"He's the best," Peter Stern, another dealer, agreed. "He's writing a Beerbohm bibliography."

Mark Samuels Lasner was certainly the real thing. In addition to Max, Peter told us that he was probably the number-one authority on Aubrey Beardsley. With his longtime associate Margaret Stetz, a professor at Georgetown, Lasner had privately published a tongue-in-cheek bibliography of Enoch Soames, in which he claimed to have made up almost nothing. He had been at the British Museum for the Soames anniversary, of course. His collection of Beerbohmiana was reputed to be among the most extensive in the world and included an original of a Soames caricature.

The first thing he asked us when we got him on the telephone was that we talk about Max and not him. We'll try but Mark Samuels Lasner is too interesting to leave out altogether.

It turned out that he was coming to New York for the Antiquarian Book Fair and he agreed to meet us for coffee at eleven o'clock at the Regency Hotel on Park Avenue and 61st Street. He could only give us an hour because he had an appointment at noon around the corner at the Grolier Club.

The Regency could not have been a better choice. We were going to meet in the part of the restaurant they call the Library. There were overstuffed sofas and chairs set up among the bookshelves and backgammon tables. The columns were even painted to look like giant Easton Press leather-bound books—*The Great Gatsby, The Adventures of Huckleberry Finn, The Grapes of Wrath*—that sort of thing.

When we got there, we didn't see any eccentric elderly men waiting for us. We walked past a dark-haired man who seemed to be in his early forties waiting at the door and asked for Mr. Lasner in the Library. They didn't know Mr. Lasner so we walked out past the same man and checked out the lobby. Finally, when we noticed that the man at the door of the restaurant didn't seem to be going anywhere, we walked up and asked if he was Mark Samuels Lasner.

"Yes," he said, smiling. "I thought the clothes would give me away." He was wearing a gray suit and tie and a Burberry-type raincoat and carrying a fedora or a homburg or something. He was indeed very Max-like, which we had entirely failed to notice.

We sat at a corner table between two large bookcases on which were displayed photographs of celebrities like Regis Philbin, George Steinbrenner, and Eartha Kitt, ordered some coffee, and began to talk about Max.

"Max Beerbohm is one of the great underrated figures in twentieth-century arts and letters," Mark began. "There's even a name for what happens to collectors who fall for Max; it's called Max-a-Mania. You see, Max is a window or doorway into an entire period, from the mid-Victorian era to the 1920s. From Max you can get to almost everyone in that period. He knew them, or he caricatured them. That's one of the reasons I'm doing his bibliography. For example, he wrote four-hundred-and-fifty-odd drama articles. I'm doing an index of every play and figure mentioned, so that if you are interested in someone in particular, you don't have to go through every article to find out what you're looking for."

We wondered if a collector of this magnitude had gotten interested in books in the same way as did every other bibliophile.

"I was a budding book collector when I was taken by a friend to meet Simon Nowell Smith, the director of the British lending library," said Mark. "He had a major Henry James collection, which is now in Canada. He collected primarily poetry—Wordsworth through Robert Graves. He had privately printed books. He had a copy of Keats's poem inscribed by his brother to his fiancée.

"I had never met a private person who owned these kinds of things. And I thought, that's incredible. I had not realized that private people collected books like this. I had no idea that you could still get these kinds of books. Then I can remember buying *The Art of Thomas Hardy,* inscribed by John Lane to George Meredith. That's the kind of book I want.

"I've practically never seen a nineteenth-century book I didn't want. For me, it's association items," said Mark. "Obviously books, but also letters, manuscripts. Having the physical object that reveals something about the author's past. I want to hold in my hand something the author actually riffled through. For me, it's the connection from one person—generally the person who made the book—to someone who owned it. It's a strange feeling. It's a different way of collecting. I have a friend who only wants to collect a book if it is in precisely the condition it would have been if he had walked into a bookshop and bought it at the time it was first issued. If I said to him that I had a copy of a book published in Paris in 1924, with a blue binding, signed by the author, but it was a little worn, he'd say, 'I'm not interested.'"

Like most serious book people, Mark is not entirely enthusiastic about current collecting trends.

"I went to the New York Antiquarian Book Fair preview last night. What people seem to want to own today are popular-culture artifacts. Dick and Jane books from the fifties, for example, go for three to four hundred dollars. The first of the three Harry Potter books is selling for $17,500. These items are very approachable—you don't have to explain them to people—and many of them have an instant visual appeal. A pretty book in an obvious dust jacket, like *The Great Gatsby*—that's what people want.

"But I'm different. I bought my first caricature in 1979. It came up at Sotheby's—an illustrated book sale, I believe. It's entitled 'Had Shakespeare Asked Me?' and shows Frank Harris, naked and rotund, standing next to a kind of shivery-looking Shakespeare. Harris, who was Max's editor at the *Saturday Review,* had written a book called *The Man Shakespeare,* which he, Harris, considered the definitive work on the subject. The story behind this caricature—it's recounted in David Cecil's biography—is that Max and Harris and a number of other people were dining altogether one day and Harris, in a loud voice, said: 'I know nothing of the joys of unnatural vice—you'd have to ask Oscar about that'—Oscar being Wilde and in prison at the time—'but had *Shakespeare* asked me, I would have had to submit.' Max went home from that dinner and immediately drew the caricature.

"I bought many of his letters as well. They're like Wilde's and Henry James's and Shaw's—even the shortest letter has appeal, even one where he just says he's so sorry he can't make it—they are all so attractive. I have one where he is apologizing for not replying sooner, because he used the original letter as a bookmark—such a charming excuse! I'm often tempted to use it myself.

"As with most collectors," Mark went on, "things eventually got out of hand. Now, it would not be an exaggeration to say that I have the largest private collection of Max Beerbohm. In fact, I've become something of a walking Beerbohm encyclopedia. For example, did you know that there were sequels to *Zuleika Dobson* written by others? What happened to Zuleika when she went to Cambridge . . . what if it was Cambridge, Massachusetts? And there was another about Zuleika during the Cold War in Moscow. There was even a plan for the Gershwins and Jerome Kern to make a musical of the original. Audrey Hepburn had the film rights for a while. She would have been perfect."

Our hour was almost up. We were waiting, hoping that, as he left for the Grolier Club, Mark Samuels Lasner would stop and say, "Oh yes. If you're ever in my neck of the woods, why don't you stop in? I'd love to show you my collection."

"But, if you want to see some of Max's work, why not go over to the Beinecke?" Mark said instead. "They've got the original manuscript of 'Enoch Soames,'" he added wistfully.

The Beinecke, of course, is the Rare Book and Manuscript Library at Yale University. According to legend (and the *Guide to the Collections* pamphlet), this library had its origins in 1701, when ten local clergymen arrived at what was then Yale College bearing an arm-load of books each. These were then handed over to the provost, or whoever was in charge at the time, accompanied by ten speeches along the lines of, "I give these books for the founding of a College in the Colony."

From this humble, theological beginning has grown one of the world's preeminent private collections. By 1742 the school had amassed twenty-six hundred volumes, including illuminated manuscripts and early printed books by Aldus; by 1930 the collection was large enough to occupy its own room at the Sterling Memorial Library; and by 1963 it had outgrown even the Sterling and had to be ensconced in its own brand-new building, renamed in honor of its benefactors.

To give a sense of the breadth of the collection is difficult. It might be easier to ask what they *don't* have. Still, in the interests of book people everywhere, here is a very small representative sampling, alphabetically, according to the catalog (not counting other related but separately housed collections, like the Medical History Library or the theological collection):

- The private papers of James Boswell;
- The Map Collection, consisting of over 200,000 map sheets and over two thousand pre-1900 atlases;
- Over three hundred editions of *Robinson Crusoe;*
- Manuscripts, first editions, and correspondence of George Eliot, including her school notebook, composed when she was fourteen;
- The Elizabethan Club collection (three hundred volumes of sixteenth- and seventeenth-century literature, including First Folios), housed separately in a vault at "the Clubhouse";
- Eleven thousand books, 850 pamphlets, four hundred broadsides, and a large group of manuscripts by or about Benjamin Franklin;
- Over thirty-one hundred incunabula, with an emphasis on Greek and Latin classics, biblical literature, Hebrew printing and German monastic bindings;

- More than eleven hundred medieval and Renaissance codices;
- Over 100,000 documents relating to the Spinellis, a distinguished Florentine family whose lineage can be traced from the fourteenth through the eighteenth century;
- The world's largest collection of Robert Louis Stevenson memorabilia, including his baby book and a scrapbook account of *Treasure Island.*

There's also a whole collection of American literature and another of western Americana; a superlative German collection, heavy on Goethe; and the Osborn Collection, given to the university by James Marshall and Marie-Louis Osborn, inspired by the eighteenth-century scholar-collector Edmond Malone. This last collection, which came to Yale at the end of the 1950s packed in two hundred liquor cartons—hmm, there's a story there—focuses on English literature from Mary Tudor to Queen Victoria.

We called ahead to make an appointment and were told that a woman named Christa Sammons was responsible for public relations.

We got to the Yale campus at about eleven o'clock and looked around for the Beinecke, or at least someone to help us find the Beinecke. Unfortunately, there was a freak April snowstorm that morning, and in addition to the large white flakes swirling around, the temperature was what television meteorologists cheerfully refer to as "unseasonably chilly." In fact, it was freezing. Yale students, being generally of a higher intelligence, were nowhere to be seen outdoors.

As we passed one of the little plazas that intersect the main quadrangle, we did see one hardy student wearing a sandwich board. It was done in crudely formed letters in blue marker, and read:

Wilkins for
Student Body President
A fresh new face

The young man wearing the sandwich board was tall and thin, wearing a coat, knit cap, and indefatigable smile. We asked for directions to the Beinecke, and he pointed the way to the building.

"Are you Wilkins?" we asked.

The young man turned and pointed to another tall and thin young man, this one hatless, wearing only jeans and a sweatshirt. "That's our man there," he said.

Wilkins smiled as we walked his way.

"Wilkins," we said. "That's a real supporter you've got there."

Wilkins nodded. "You can't vote, can you?" he asked, showing that old Yale know-how.

"Sorry," we replied.

We hurried off to our appointment. It was a cold day to be Wilkins. But it will probably serve him well. We expect to see Wilkins as that fresh new face in the United States Senate twenty years from now.

The Beinecke was not what we were expecting. Although the brochure refers to the architects' claim that the library forms "a strong and complementary relationship with the other buildings" facing onto Yale's Hewitt Quadrangle, on a campus filled with ivy-covered Gothic architecture, the windowless Beinecke stands out like a giant monolithic sculpture, the kind of thing you'd expect to see in a Hollywood film about a futuristic fascist government brought down by Will Smith. Inside, the decor is the same, with marble stairs, iron railings, and six-story honeycomb outer walls interlaced with huge marble panels. The books are enclosed in a rectangular glass case—all six floors of them. You can walk around and see them from every angle. It's a box within a box.

As we went through the front door, we saw a large desk manned by a single very serious-looking gray-uniformed security officer. He lifted his head and eyed us as we walked over. We told him that we had an appointment, but instead of reaching for his telephone to dial Christa Sammons's extension, he reached under the desk and came up with a big rectangular piece of rock.

"This is an exact piece of the marble they used for the panels," he said, handing it over to us. "It's the exact thickness. An inch and a half."

We held it. It was heavy.

"It comes from Danby, Vermont," the security guard continued. We had the feeling that he whipped this piece of marble out anytime someone new walked in the door. "Two hundred and sixty panels each weighing about nine hundred pounds. The panels were installed in the succession in which they were cut, so the lines in the marble vary only slightly from panel to panel."

We nodded. "Do you show this to everyone who walks in?" we asked.

"Sure," he said. "They're translucent, by the way. On a sunny day, they turn orange."

As the guard continued to regale us with other tales of the building's construction, a thin, studious-looking woman with short gray hair and glasses appeared at the top of the stairway that led to the lower level. She was wearing a black skirt, very hip patterned black stockings, and low-heeled shoes.

Christa Sammons, it turned out, was the curator of the German Literature Collection. "There are six curators," she explained, "and each of us gets an added job. Mine is publicity."

She took us downstairs to her office. As we walked through the hallway of the administrative area, we passed some museum-caliber portraits. "Our gifts often come with art," she said, gesturing to the paintings on the wall. "It's one of the advantages of working here."

Christa had a good-sized office, but it was so stuffed with books, papers, and catalogs that it felt cramped. We sat down and she got right to it.

"There were three Beinecke brothers, Edwin, Frederick, and Walter. Only Frederick graduated from Yale. Edwin collected medieval manuscripts, illuminated manuscripts—the pretty kind—and

Robert Louis Stevenson. We have the world's largest Robert Louis
Stevenson collection. We have his manuscripts, his library, his letters. We have his *tapa* quilt. It's mounted on the wall in the lobby.
We have an incredible painting of him too. You might have noticed
it—it's right down the hall. He looks really sexy. I'm not sure he
really looked like that, though. I've seen other likenesses of him and
he always looks thinner and more sickly.

"In any event, Edwin collected Stevenson and Frederick collected western Americana. Walter died before the building was
opened. I think he was the number cruncher. They were the S and
H Green Stamp Corporation, you know. Do you remember S and
H Green Stamps in the fifties when they were so popular? It was big
business. Old immigrant granddaddy Beinecke was a butcher who
eventually supplied wholesale meats to New York. Then he got into
construction, like the Plaza Hotel. The Green Stamp business was
owned by one of the in-laws, but the Beineckes developed it, made
it what it was.

"Walter wrote the rules for bridge. He was a big bridge player.
He was also an excellent chess player. He and Granddaddy would
play a game of chess and they wouldn't use a board."

She moved quickly from the brothers to the collection.

"Our strengths are in the humanities. We have medieval manuscripts. We're very strong in eighteenth-century British literature—
Johnson, Boswell, that sort of thing. We're strong in the Victorian
period, in British periodicals. We have a huge strength in twentieth-
century modernism. We have a wonderful German literature section, particularly the baroque period and the age of Goethe. We
have Edith Wharton manuscripts and dozens of photographs of her
in her garden, in her study, with her dogs. . . .

"This isn't a fortress," she continued. "We're a part of Yale, of
course, and our main obligation is to the university but anyone with
a real interest is encouraged to use the Beinecke. Sometimes we
send people away if they're just looking because our materials are so
specific that you need to have done some research before you use

them—you know, to have read a biography or something. But all you need to use the library are two pieces of identification."

She smiled. "Some of our materials attract a different kind of person. The Voynich Manuscript, for instance. That's a late-fifteenth-century/early-sixteenth-century manuscript in cipher. No one's ever cracked the cipher. There are Internet sites about it. It looks like some kind of medical manuscript. It has pictures of little naked ladies flying around on what look like tubes of toothpaste. Then there's the original copy of the Book of Mormon. We have whole contingents come down to look at that."

We asked who some of the Beinecke's competitors were for acquisitions and she mentioned a number of places including the Harry Ransom Library at the University of Texas.

"Oh yes, they have a lot of money," we observed.

Christa's face set and her voice dropped a little. "*We* have a lot of money," she said evenly.

We asked about the architecture—it was impossible not to.

"The Beinecke has been called 'a jewel box,'" Christa said, "but that's the opposite of how we want it to be viewed. We want to be viewed as a welcoming place, a helpful place, an institution in the forefront of acquisition.

"Of course," she admitted, "it can be kind of . . . forbidding. I was a graduate student here in the sixties and I never set foot inside."

Actually, it turned out not to be forbidding at all. The people behind the desk were cordial and helpful. They showed us how to sign in, how to use the computerized catalog, and how to request materials from the stacks. They set us up in their files so that the process could be expedited the next time we came to pester them. They even smiled.

The Max Beerbohm Collection, we saw from the computer listing, came in two boxes. We filled out a request, waited about five minutes, then picked up the boxes and took them across the hall to the reading room.

The reading room was behind glass doors and was outfitted with long tables. There were several other people in there, but it was completely quiet. Even the people using laptops seemed to hit the keys without making a sound.

We found the "Enoch Soames" manuscript immediately. It was prefaced by a sheet of paper that read:

THE AUTHOR'S ORIGINAL MANUSCRIPT WITH
THREE PAGES OF DRAWINGS

23. BEERBOHM (Sir Max).
ENOCH SOAMES
A MEMORY OF THE EIGHTEEN-NINETIES
BY MAX BEERBOHM
(The original Autograph Manuscript)
25 leaves, folio, with many deletions and corrections, neatly written in ink; with marginal instructions to the typist in pencil; the reverse of three leaves contain characteristic pencil drawings by the Author
L 165

This manuscript was presented by the Author to the British Red Cross Sale at Christie's, July, 1940. On a separate sheet Sir Max Beerbohm had written:

For the Red Cross, 1940
from Max Beerbohm—
Ms. of story
entitled "Enoch Soames,"
and published in
volume entitled
"Seven Men" (1919)

The manuscript was written on thick, stiff, unlined, almost legal-size paper, which we found out later was drawing paper. The handwriting was delicate, small, and precise, in black ink with lots of cross-outs and inserts. When Max Beerbohm crossed out, he *really* crossed out, blotting out whole passages so that you couldn't tell what was there before, as if whatever it was had been so unsuitable that any reminder had to be obliterated entirely from the work. The manuscript included three caricatures that had apparently been drawn at the time of writing, a way to flesh out the characters, to make them real—or perhaps they were real to Max and he was simply putting them down on paper as he saw them. The first, on the back of page three, was of Enoch Soames standing, smoking a cigarette in his waterproof cape and low, wide-brimmed hat. Rothenstein is sitting in the background at a table wearing a top hat, tie, and eyeglasses. Enoch Soames's shoulders droop and his body hangs forward as though he already knows that he will not find his name in the Reading Room one hundred years hence. On the back of page six there is another caricature of Soames, this time in profile, a cigarette dangling from his lips. He is minus the hat, but still wearing his cape. His fingers are long, effeminate, supercilious— the drawings are both charming and damning at the same time.

It was very interesting to see the original portraits of Soames. In our copy of *Seven Men* there are also caricatures of Soames, but in these later, published versions, Max has made Soames much more pitiable. The stooping shoulders and blank face have been accentuated and all the original smugness and chutzpah are missing. We wondered if Max, after finishing the piece and dooming the man to perdition, had decided to take it just a bit easier on poor Soames.

On the back of page twelve is the Devil. We could tell that Max had a lot of fun with this one. Satan is depicted as a large, robust, barrel-chested man, standing straight and tall, confident, with a large nose, a goatee, a vest, and a cravat. He's unmistakably the Devil, but he might just as easily be an industrialist—or a theater manager. There were penciled notes to the typist in Max's distinctive hand sprinkled throughout the manuscript. Here's the one he wrote about the reference Soames found on that fateful afternoon in 1997:

To Typist
*Please be
careful to
get this phonetic
spelling right
—though I
admit that
this is asking
rather much!*
MB

Max signed each of his notes "MB" as though, without the initials, there might have been some confusion as to the source of the instruction.

We went through the rest of the first box. There was also an autograph manuscript of "No. 2, The Pines," one of Max's most famous essays, about visiting Algernon Swinburne. It was written at the behest of Edmund Gosse, who had wanted a few words for a biography. This was too difficult for Max—"I found it hard to be brief without seeming irreverent. I failed in the attempt to make of my subject a snapshot that was not a grotesque"—so instead he wrote an entire essay, recalling a number of times he had visited Swinburne at his address at No. 2, The Pines, in Putney, a suburb of London.

"No. 2, The Pines" is notable both for its portrait of a famous man at the end of his career and for Max's delicious sense of humor. Swinburne is introduced frankly as a genius whose best work is behind him—"The essential Swinburne was still the earliest," Max wrote. By the time of Max's first visit, Swinburne is an old man:

It is true that Swinburne did, from time to time, take public notice of current affairs; but what notice he took did but seem to mark his remoteness from them, from us. The Boers, I remember, were the theme of a sonnet which embarrassed even their angriest enemies in our midst. He likened them, if I remember rightly, to "hell-hounds foaming at the jaws." This was by some people taken as a sign that he had fallen away from that high generosity of spirit which had once been his.

Max never sees Swinburne except in the company of Theodore Watts-Dunton, another old man and close friend of Dante Gabriel Rossetti, who has taken upon himself the responsibility for the poet's welfare. Both Swinburne and Watts-Dunton are deaf, so Watts-Dunton roars at Max and Max shouts back; lunch always consists of roast mutton and apple pie; Watts-Dunton doesn't let Swinburne talk until he feels Swinburne has eaten enough to sustain him until dinner. Yet "I loved those sessions in that Tupperossettine dining-room," wrote Max, who regularly made up descriptive words to suit his purposes when he felt that ordinary English prose fell short.

"No. 2, The Pines," like "Enoch Soames," was on unlined drawing paper and contained caricatures of the story's participants—in this case, Swinburne, Whistler, and Watts-Dunton. Max had even drawn himself as a young man among the sketches of Swinburne. He looked very young, respectful, and a little bit afraid, which is how he portrayed himself in the essay:

> On the day appointed "I came as one whose feet half linger." It is but a few steps from the railway-station in Putney High Street to No. 2 The Pines. I had expected a greater distance to the sanctuary—a walk in which to compose my mind and prepare myself for initiation. I laid my hand irresolutely against the gate of the bleak trim front-garden, I withdrew my hand, I went away. Out here were all the aspects of common modern life. In there was Swinburne. A butcher-boy went by, whistling. He was not going to see Swinburne. He could afford to whistle.

It is also in "No. 2, The Pines" that Max gives perhaps the best explanation of his own appeal in describing the appeal of another. He writes of Theodore Watts-Dunton:

> It was always when Watts-Dunton spoke carelessly, casually, of some to me illustrious figure in the past, that I had the sense of being wafted right into that past and plumped down in the very midst of it. When he spoke with reverence of this and that great man whom he had known, he did not thus waft and plump me; for I, too, revered those names. But I had the magical transition whenever one of the immortals was mentioned in the tone of those who knew him before he had put on immortality. Browning, for example, was a name deeply honoured by me. "Browning, yes," said Watts-Dunton, in the course of an afternoon, "Browning," and he took a sip of the steaming whisky-toddy that was a point in our day's ritual. "I was a great diner-out in the old times. I used to dine out every night in the week. Browning was a great diner-out, too. We were always meeting. What a pity he went on writing all those plays! He hadn't any gift for drama—none. I never could understand why he took to play-writing." He wagged his head, gazing regretfully into the fire, and added, "Such a *clever* fellow, too!"

And that's just what Max with all his essays and stories and caricatures does . . . George Bernard Shaw, Oscar Wilde, Frank Harris, Aubrey Beardsley, Lytton Strachey, Rudyard Kipling . . . he knew them all before they put on immortality, so he wafts and plumps us down in their midst. "Henry James, yes," you can almost hear him say.

After we put "No. 2, The Pines" back carefully in the box, we leafed through the rest of the collection. Someone had donated letters as well. One in particular backed up Mark Samuels Lasner's observations of Max's correspondence. It was written on a piece of hotel stationery with a picture of an imposing seaside resort at the top labeled "GRANDS ESTABLISSEMENTS/DES BAINS ET DU CASINO/DE BOULOGNE-SUR-MER":

Boulogne-S/Mer, October 1, 1897
Dear Sir
    I have not, as you have, the good fortune to be a writer of fiction—so I can trust you to believe in the following apology and excuse for what may have seemed to you, some months ago, my discourtesy. By this time, you have probably forgotten that you ever wrote to me—Let me recall to your memory that you did write to me a letter in which you said some very pleasant things about one of my articles in the "Daily Mail" and in which you asked whether I would publish a book through the firm of Mr. Bowden. My knowledge of the letter dates from this morning. In the breast pocket of an overcoat, which I had not worn since the early months of this year, I was startled at finding three unopened envelopes. One of them contained a bill, another a letter of no great importance, and the last your letter. . . .
    Since this morning I have made excavations in all my other pockets. . . .
    Believe me

                                            Yours very truly
                                            Max Beerbohm

We put the letters back, walked out of that silent reading room, and returned the boxes to the front desk. It was just as Mark Samuels Lasner had said: there was something about touching a piece of paper that you knew Max himself had handled, seeing it as he had seen it, that establishes a connection far deeper than is possible from just reading his work.

In the Round Reading Room of the British Museum, at precisely 2:10 P.M. on June 3, 1997, a man really did appear. He was sporting, according to Nigel Reynolds, crack reporter for the *London Daily Telegraph,* "a 19th-century cleric's hat, and a grey cloak." According to another observer, Teller of Penn and Teller, writing in the *Atlantic Monthly,* "The wide brimmed beaver hat is threadbare. The cape is mud-stained. The man under the cape appears to be in his late twenties, with a large head, long neck, and sloping shoulders. He is pale save for scattered inflammations on his skin, and his mouse-brown hair droops down his neck."

According to authoritative accounts, the figure moved to the appropriate catalog section, then, obviously not finding what he was looking for, inquired at the center desk. Soon after, the caped man disappeared without a trace.

"You know Soames actually did appear in 1997 at the British Reading Room," we were told by an attendee. "Actually, two Soameses appeared. The first was an actor. He was exposed almost immediately but no one knows who hired him. The second was a genuine apparition. It was very hazy and kind of floated around like a hologram. I think Teller of Penn and Teller had something to do with it. That evening, there was a small celebration. There was wine and champagne. Some people came in period costume. Soames's poems were read. It was quite nice."

The very next year, the Round Reading Room was torn apart and completely renovated.

"The renovation had been planned since the seventies," Mark Samuels Lasner noted, "but they kept putting it off. Everyone who was there that day is convinced that the reason the renovation didn't take place sooner, as it was scheduled to, was to allow Soames to appear in the original setting as predicted."

Chapter 3

THE NEW ENGLAND FORGER

On Friday, April 3, 1998, at a small country auction in Sheffield, Massachusetts, the following item was offered for sale:

> B38
> 1VOL (*SIGNED BY POUND AND YEATS*) Pound Ezra (Editor) "Passages from the Letters of John Butler Yeats: Selected by Ezra Pound" Churchtown (Cuala Press), 1917. 8 VO. 1st Edition 1 of 400 copies. This copy is signed on the colophon page by Yeats and Pound.
> Blue-gray boards and cloth with paper label printed in black; lightly soiled. Lacks front free end-paper. This combination of signatures is very rare.
>
> $500–750

The book in question was a slim, unassuming volume, only sixty-one pages. It was in generally fine condition, except for the missing blue front free endpaper, which is the first page (usually blank or decorative) that the reader sees upon opening the cover. The auction house, Bradford Galleries, whose main line of business was estate sales—furniture, rugs, china, and knick-knacks—had accepted the book on consignment from Randy Weinstein, a rare-book dealer up the road in Great Barrington. Although Weinstein had been collecting privately for years, he had only just opened his shop, North Star Rare Books & Manuscripts, and was new to the sales side of the book business. For a year and a half before opening the business, he had traveled all over the area, buying up books to stock his shop. Somewhere along the way Weinstein had picked up the Yeats for about two hundred dollars. Because it had been damaged, he wasn't quite sure what it was worth, so he put it up for auction.

Small country auctions like this one have always been a prime hunting ground in the antiquarian book trade. Valuable books and manuscripts have a habit of popping up from people's old shoeboxes or out of garages, attics, or carriage houses. A packet of Melville letters and a *Typee* manuscript were discovered in just this way right next door in upstate New York in 1983. Of course, the story everyone in the antiquarian book business knows, which was made famous by John Dunning in his mystery classic *Booked To Die,* is the copy of *Tamerlane* by "A Bostonian," unearthed at a New England tag sale for five dollars, which turned out to be Edgar Allan Poe's first book, and which subsequently sold at auction at Sotheby's for a quarter of a million.

When Jim Cummins noticed item B38 in the Bradford catalog, he was immediately interested. An easygoing, affable man, Jim has been a bookseller for nearly thirty years. His shop, James Cummins Rare Books, occupies the entire top floor of a seven-story building on Madison Avenue in the low 60s in Manhattan, one of the most expensive locations in the world. His shelves are filled with leather-bound sets from famous binders, rare first editions, and elegant drawings by nineteenth-century artists such as Dante Gabriel Rossetti. Jim caters to an impressive international clientele that includes Hollywood movie stars Johnny Depp and Ricky Jay.

After he read the catalog description, Jim made a phone call to his friend and fellow dealer Terry Halladay at William Reese Company in New Haven, Connecticut. Terry, a tall, angular, intense man, had a long history with Pound, having worked extensively with both the Pound archives at the Beinecke and the New Directions archive at Harvard. What's more, he was a Yeats collector himself.

The Yeats in question was William Butler Yeats, John Butler Yeats's much more famous Nobel Prize–winning son, and the editor of the entire Cuala Press series. Terry had never seen a book signed by both Pound and Yeats, although Pound had been Yeats's secretary from 1912 to 1914. The closest Terry had come to having both of their signatures on the same page was the letter he had purchased in London in 1987 for $1200, which had been dictated by Yeats to Pound (who wrote it out in longhand), with Yeats then signing underneath. Both Terry and Jim were well aware that another Cuala Press book, *The Wild Swans at Coole,* which was inscribed by Yeats to Pound, and which, like *Passages,* was one of only four hundred copies, had sold at auction in California in 1994 for $12,000.

Terry and Jim decided to throw in together on *Passages,* a common practice among dealers for spreading risk. Even though the book had been valued by Bradford at only $500–$750, there was no telling who else might have seen the catalog and therefore how high the bids might go. If they succeeded in buying the book, one or the other would then list it in his catalog, depending upon whose customer base was judged to have the higher percentage of potential Yeats or Pound collectors. When it sold, they'd split the profits.

Before the actual bidding, as a final precaution they called Rusty Mott and asked him to run over and have a look at the book during the preview. Rusty, a big, red-headed man, ran Howard S. Mott Rare Books out of a large colonial in Sheffield, about a five-minute drive from the Bradford Galleries. Although by no means a Pound or Yeats expert—Rusty's specialty was early Americana—he could be relied upon to judge a book's condition and to report any flaws the catalog description might have glossed over, which might in turn affect the book's overall salability. Ideally, collectors and dealers look for books and manuscripts in perfect condition; "as new" it's called. Any deterioration from that standard will reflect in the price.

Rusty, who performed this sort of service regularly for out-of-town dealers, agreed to have a look at *Passages*. He reported that the book was in the condition described and that the two signatures did appear on the last page as stated.

And so, when Item B38 was offered at Bradford's that Friday, the high bidder, by telephone, was Jim Cummins.

He got it for $850.

Two weeks later, the New York Antiquarian Book Fair opened at the Seventh Regiment Armory on Park Avenue in Manhattan.

The New York Antiquarian Book Fair is generally considered to be the most important annual event in the rare-book trade. It is the place where the world's finest books are offered by the world's most prestigious dealers, often at the world's highest prices. For the 1998 fair, for example, Heritage Book Shop of Los Angeles, California, brought Edmund Spenser's *The Faerie Queene,* London 1590, *The Second Part of the Faerie Queene,* London, 1596, and Book of Hours, in Latin, illuminated manuscript on vellum, southwest France, late fifteenth century. Simon Finch of London, booksellers for over two hundred years, had a pristine copy of Sir Isaac Newton's *Philosophiae Naturalis Principia Mathematica.* Boston's Bromer Booksellers brought letters written by Ernest Hemingway. There were autographed musical manuscripts by Wagner and Schubert, first editions of Dickens and Sir Francis Bacon, and *The Workes of Sir Thomas More Knyght, sometyme Lorde Chauncellour of England, wrytten by him in the Englysh tonge,* London, 1557, first collected edition in folio. To rent the smallest booth at this fair costs over $3000. But it's worth it. It is rumored that a dealer once sold $450,000 worth of books in a single day.

It was to this fair that Jim Cummins brought his newly purchased, double-signed *Passages from the Letters of John Butler Yeats: Selected by Ezra Pound.*

As soon as he could, Jim brought the book over to Terry Halladay, who immediately opened to the back and examined the signatures. Sure enough, there on the colophon (a printed inscription on the last page of the book stating facts relating to the publishing and printing of the work) were "W.B. Yeats," and, immediately underneath, "Ezra Pound." There was a blot over the first letters of both signatures, which had left a small stain on the preceding page. The signatures were each about a half-inch high, and looked to have been written with the same black fountain pen.

Terry frowned. There was something odd about the Pound signature . . . the book was a presentation copy from the 1920s, but the signature was reminiscent of the way Ezra Pound would have signed his name much later in life, say around the 1960s. There was an extended tail on the "d," which was a lot sloppier than Pound would have been when he was younger. Also, the "P" should have had more of a flourish. The whole signature, now that Terry looked at it carefully, was somehow too considered, too hesitant; there was a lack of fluidity about it. Also, both signatures were written with the same pen, which, while of course possible, seemed nonetheless unusual.

Troubled by the overall look of the colophon, Terry turned the book over in his hands. There were threads standing up from the binding—the book might have been resewn. The missing front endpaper had been cut away cleanly, as though it had been razored out. If someone had torn off a piece to write down a telephone number or something, part of the page would still have been there, and the tear would have been ragged. There was no telling what had been on that page before. It could have held a library stamp, or someone's bookplate . . . In Terry's experience, when a book had been altered in this way, it was usually because someone was trying to hide something.

"Something's not right here," he told Jim.

Wanting someone with whom to confer, Terry looked around for another expert. After all, no single dealer can know everything. Ordinarily, a conference of this type would have taken weeks as the book was examined and shipped back and forth between shops. But this was the New York Antiquarian Book Fair. Most of the major dealers in Ezra Pound and W. B. Yeats were milling around a few seconds' walk away.

Terry chose his friend Ed Maggs, of Maggs Brothers of London, one of the best-known and most prestigious rare-book dealers in the world. Maggs Brothers has been around since the 1850s. It has traded on behalf of kings and queens, and intermediated in passing antiquarian treasures among the world's richest men. Maggs's letterhead carries a very British seal, underneath which is printed:

**By Appointment To
Her Majesty The Queen
Purveyors Of Rare Books
& Manuscripts Maggs Bros., London**

Terry handed the book to Ed and asked him to have a look at it. After a short examination, Ed Maggs rendered his verdict.

It was the same as Terry's. The signatures were forgeries.

Although the word *forgery* is more likely to bring to mind a bank document or fake Picasso than a T. S. Eliot first edition, the antiquarian book market has always had its share of scoundrels. In the nineteenth century, for example, an English businessman named Thomas J. Wise, who was also a noted bibliophile, took to surreptitiously printing little Victorian pamphlets under the names of people like Elizabeth Barrett Browning and selling them at a profit to other collectors. When these documents were found to have been composed of materials unavailable in the years in which they were purportedly printed, Wise forfeited all of his legitimate accomplishments in bibliography and died a broken man.

Most recently, America has been the site of two celebrated book forgery scams, one vaguely comical but both of them deadly. The first involved two Texas good ol' boy book dealers, C. Dorman David and John H. Jenkins. In the early 1970s, Jenkins ran the most prestigious rare-book operation in the Lone Star State but, with David's assistance, supplemented his income with homemade early Texana documents like this famous William Barret Travis call to arms of 1836:

To the People of Texas & all Americans *in the World*—
Fellow citizens & compatriots—
 I am besieged, by a thousand or more of the Mexicans under Santa Anna—I have sustained a continual bombardment & cannonade for 24 hours & have not lost a man—The enemy has demanded a surrender at discretion, otherwise, the garrison are to be put to the sword, if the fort is taken—I have answered the demand with a cannon shot, & our flag still waves proudly from the walls—*I shall never surrender or retreat. Then,* I call on you in the name of Liberty, of patriotism & every thing dear to the American character, to come to our aid, with all dispatch—The enemy is receiving reinforcements daily & will no doubt increase to three or four thousand in four or five days. If this call is neglected, I am determined to sustain myself as long as possible & die like a soldier who never forgets what is due to his own honor & that of his country—

Victory or Death
William Barret Travis
Lt. Col. comdt

As a result of Messrs. David and Jenkins's efforts, so many "originals" of this tract became available to the public at large that they could be found framed on the walls of dentists' offices. In fact, this was the very letter that was read by George W. Bush to members of the 1999 United States Ryder Cup Golf Team as a morale booster the night before their remarkable comeback against the Europeans. One wonders where he got his copy.

Like a number of other forgers, Messrs. David and Jenkins did not limit their activities to forgery; they stole, too. In *Texfake: An Account of the Theft and Forgery of Early Texas Printed Documents,* the author, W. Thomas Taylor, himself a book dealer who was instrumental in catching these two varmints, describes an auction that took place in a ballroom in Houston:

> . . . featuring seventy-seven glittering pieces of historical Texana "From the Collection of C. Dorman David." An introduction to the catalog proclaimed that "[David] has one of the largest collections of Texana in the world," which he was able to form because he "collected Texas manuscripts when they were rarely sold to the public." This was true: they were rarely sold to the public because the public owned them in the first place.

David was eventually caught and sent to jail, although it was for theft and narcotics trafficking, not forgery. Jenkins's end was as flamboyant as his career, which had included, of all things, a stint as a security officer and then one as president of the Antiquarian Booksellers Association of America. He was found dead of a gunshot wound in 1989. The circumstances remain a mystery. Some say that Jenkins was rubbed out because he was deeply in debt to gamblers (he had once competed in the World Series of Poker), others that he was simply sufficiently obnoxious to inspire someone to blow his brains out. The local sheriff, however, ruled Jenkins's death a suicide despite the fact that he was shot in the back of the head and no gun was found at the scene.

There were no doubts about causes of death in the other forgery case. In 1985, Mark W. Hofmann, a thirty-one-year-old lapsed Mormon with a wife and two small children, killed two people in Salt Lake City, Utah, in an attempt to cover his tracks as a book and document forger. His most notorious "discovery"—which turned out to be a complete fabrication—was the 1830 "Salamander Letter" in which Mormon leader Joseph Smith "claimed that an angel revealed the location of buried gold plates, which Smith translated into the Book of Mormon . . . this early letter recounted how a white salamander, guarding the plates, transformed itself into an 'old spirit,' struck Smith three times, and forbade him to take the ancient treasure."* Hofmann was in the process of selling fictitious papers of renegade Mormon apostle William McLellin to the Mormon Church for $185,000 when, fearful of discovery, he planted two pipe bombs. The first killed Steve Christensen, a financial consultant and Mormon bishop who was supposed to authenticate the McLellin collection. The second was aimed at Christensen's old boss, Gary Sheets, whose investment company was in trouble and rumored to have Mafia connections. This bomb, which was meant as a decoy to throw suspicion off the McLellin transaction, was left in Sheets's driveway and was mistakenly picked up by his wife, Kathy, who died instantly.

Unlike C. Dorman David and John H. Jenkins, flamboyant conmen who dealt in relatively inexpensive items in quantity, $5,000 or so at a time, Mark Hofmann specialized in big, one-of-a-kind, history-making deals. The Salamander Letter went for $40,000. At the time of his arrest (he was in the act of planting a third pipe bomb when it went off in his car, wounding him and confirming

---

*Quotation is from *Salamander: The Story of the Mormon Forgery Murders* by Linda Sillitoe and Allen Roberts (Signature Books, Inc.: Salt Lake City, 1990).

police suspicions that Hofmann was in fact the bomber), he was negotiating the sale of "Oath of a Freeman" to the Library of Congress. The Library reportedly offered $1 million for this document, the first printed in the American colonies, but backed off when Hofmann demanded $1.5 million. When investigators searched his home, they found a receipt from the Argosy Bookstore in New York listing, among other inexpensive items, "Oath of a Freeman" for $25. Hofmann later claimed that the document he bought from Argosy was genuine, but it seems clear that this was merely a copy that he used as the basis for his forgery.

Both the Jenkins affair and the Mark Hofmann case made a big impression on the close-knit, secluded world of antiquarian books. For a long time, it was impossible to hear the word "forgery" without associating it with murder.

It didn't take long for a buzz to make it around the floor of the Park Avenue Armory. As *Passages from the Letters of John Butler Yeats: Selected by Ezra Pound* was passed from hand to hand, stories about a forger operating out of New England passed right along with them. Other dealers stepped forward and confirmed that they had been stung before, and other suspicious books—a couple of T. S. Eliots and a Hemingway—were found at the fair. Unlike the Pound and Yeats signatures, the Hemingway, which included a lengthy inscription, was, according to more than one dealer, "very, very good."

Inevitably, the buzz and the questionable books were brought to the attention of Priscilla Juvelis, the president of the Antiquarian Booksellers' Association of America (ABAA), the same position that John Jenkins had held over a decade before.

The ABAA was founded in 1949 at the Grolier Club in New York. Its charter members were the legendary book people of the time, who, even today, are spoken of reverentially by those in the trade. They included Jack N. Bartfield, Louis Cohen of Argosy Books, Marston Drake of James F. Drake, Inc., Howard S. Mott, Lawrence

I. Verry of Barnes and Noble, and Charles Retz of Scribners. According to "The ABAA at Fifty: Notes Toward a History of the Antiquarian Booksellers' Association of America," by Edwin V. Glaser (quoting the March 3, 1949 issue of the *Antiquarian Bookman*):

> It was recognized that there were a great many differences, a long backlog of personal disputes and dissensions and an enormous field of individual views and prejudices. It was also recognized that all the above were some of the very reasons why a national association of antiquarian booksellers had to be formed not merely to reconcile the differences but also to advance book-buying, to promote book-collecting, so that all would benefit from such increased activity in the book field. . . . In a spirited discussion led by Messrs. Verry, Gomme, Schatzki and Drake . . . it was agreed that the first major purpose would be to further book buying and collecting. Each dealer was now trying to do by himself what an organization could do far more effectively. The necessity of ethical standards was raised but it was generally agreed that this was a subsidiary purpose, which would be a natural evolution of the organization.

Over time, the ABAA created an ethics committee and the organization adopted as its objective "to encourage interest in rare books and manuscripts and to maintain the highest standards in the antiquarian book trade."

From the first, the ABAA, while titularly the rare-book world's national organization and conduit to the outside world, was in fact an organization of the higher-end, more prestigious dealers. Although not every ABAA member has a fancy shop or deals in ten-thousand-dollar books (there are many members who conduct business out of their homes), the ABAA is not easy to join. In fact, the entrance requirements are reminiscent of those for an Ivy League college. There's even an essay:

Applications require sponsorship of four current members of ABAA and three secondary sponsors, a biographical letter, a credit report, samples of catalogs or stock listings, and an Applicant Essay. There is a $50 non-refundable application fee.

Sponsors must have been ABAA members for 3 years, and can only sponsor two new members per year. One must visit the premises personally within 60 days prior to the application (Primary Sponsor). The application must be received at least 90 days prior to a Board of Governors meeting. These are held in February, April, July, and November. The application is circulated to the membership for comment, and there is usually a local interview by one current local member. The list of applicants is also published in *AB Bookmans Weekly* for public comment. A ⅔ vote of the Board is required. When accepted, there is an entrance fee of $300 and the dues are $450 per calendar year, as well as a regional chapter's dues where applicable.

All active members of ABAA are listed on the ABAA Web site as a benefit of their membership and are eligible to post catalogs.

In return for all of this, in addition to the listing on the Internet, an ABAA member receives such benefits as the right to participate at big-time ABAA book fairs (although he or she still has to pay for the booth), membership directories, cooperative bookshops, a trade publication *(The ABAA Newsletter),* and potential eligibility in a benevolent fund for needy rare-book sellers.

While the ABAA promotes itself as representing the best in the profession, not every dealer takes such a lofty view. Many midlevel and lower-end dealers, who don't have millionaire clients and cannot afford the fancy shops or the thousands of dollars it takes to rent a booth at ABAA fairs, think of ABAA members as a clubby bunch of snooty prima donnas. They view the organization as being less concerned with maintaining high standards than with maintaining high prices, especially in their segment of the market. In fact, non-ABAA members have set up shadow book fairs that run at the same time and in the same cities as ABAA-sponsored events. Not surprisingly, many ABAA members dismiss this perspective as simply a case of sour grapes.

But whichever view you favor, there is little question that the ABAA has come to epitomize the industry's class stratification, the haves versus the have-nots.

Taking advantage of the fact that just about everyone is already there, the ABAA uses the New York Antiquarian Book Fair to conduct the business of recruiting new appointees to the various ABAA committees. As it happened, the term of the current security committee chairman had just run out. Ordinarily, chairman of security is a pretty relaxed post, the main objective being to keep track of stolen books, report thefts, and publicize credit card frauds. Forgery hadn't been a problem since John Jenkins's term, and that was a whole different sort of problem, since it was the president who was the forger.

But now there was the New England forger, as he had become known in the trade, and something had to be done about him. He didn't even seem to be a member. Already the rumors were strong enough to have spread to the public. If the customers coming into the fair found out about it, they might not buy with confidence. And if they couldn't buy with confidence . . . they might not buy at all.

It was Priscilla Juvelis's job to find a new security chairman. Priscilla, who is as upstanding as John Jenkins was not, looked around for somebody who could handle a tough situation.

John Crichton is a scholarly-looking man in his fifties. He owns and operates the Brick Row Bookshop in San Francisco, which specializes in higher-end antiquarian and Americana. John is as strong an advertisement for his industry as it is possible to find. His love and knowledge of books are obvious, his selection is known across the country, and his prices are fair.

John is one of the West Coast dealers who make the annual pilgrimage to Manhattan for the book fair. He's been in the business for twenty years, and during that time has volunteered on various ABAA committees.

Priscilla had known John almost since she started her bookselling career. Casting around for a potential appointee, she remembered what a good job John had done as chairman of the membership committee back in 1988. Without actually mentioning the existence of the forger, she sounded him out as to his willingness to head up the security committee. John said okay, and just like that the forger became his problem.

"Which is why I don't usually volunteer for things," he said later.

In very short order it became clear to John Crichton that the New England forger, while a recent revelation to many ABAA dealers (or so they claimed later), was anything but new to most of the used-book dealers in western Massachusetts and Connecticut. By some accounts, the forger had been operating for almost ten years. His modus operandi, at least in the beginning, was to buy a cheap edition of a book by a well-known author, forge (with varying degrees of expertise) the signature of that author, and then resell the now-signed book at a price significantly below market value (but still at a substantial profit) to a willing dealer near his home in north central Connecticut. He often sold a number of books at once, some signed, some not, explaining to a dealer that an uncle or grandfather had died and left him a collection that he now had to sell because he needed money.

Some of the earlier forgeries were so amateurish as to be laughable but he had apparently gotten better over the years. Also, in many instances, the forger had made the almost inconceivably unprofessional mistake of blind-stamping the books with his own name. Blind-stamping makes an embossed impression on the page, like a corporate seal, except that instead of a company, the owner's name appears. Some collectors use blind-stamping in place of bookplates to indicate that a particular book has come from his or her library, although unless that collector happens to be famous, a blind stamp (or a bookplate, for that matter) immediately decreases the value of the book.

Thus, many of the forged books bore the words "From the library of Kenneth R. Anderson."

After the fair, John Crichton went back to San Francisco and tried to decide what to do next. He had been unsuccessful in finding out very much about Kenneth R. Anderson, except that he had become so brazen that he was now operating as a dealer under the name of Old Nail Books. John composed an e-mail to the ABAA membership. "I worded it carefully," he said. "I had never laid eyes on this guy, didn't know him, so I had to be careful. He may have been litigious . . . or dangerous."

The e-mail, issued on May 15, 1998, read:

MEMBER ADVISORY

On several recent occasions members of the ABAA have been offered, and in some cases purchased, books allegedly signed by T. S. Eliot, W. B. Yeats, Ernest Hemingway, Rudyard Kipling, John Steinbeck and Robert Frost, among others, from Ken Anderson, who does business as Old Nail Books in Stafford Springs, Conn. (This Ken Anderson is NOT to be confused with an ABAA member of good standing, Kenneth Andersen of Auburn, Mass.) Upon close examination the authenticity of a significant number of these autographs has been questioned and disputed by members of the ABAA who are familiar with such material. Members are advised to treat with suspicion and examine with great care any material in their inventory which came from this source and, if needed, to consult with

other qualified members of the Association as to the authenticity of the autographs.

Anyone with questions or information relative to this should
refer them to the ABAA Security Chair, John Crichton of the
Brick Row Book Shop . . .

Considering how pervasive Ken Anderson's work was reputed to
be, John got surprisingly little response to his e-mail, and most of
what he did get was anecdotal and unsubstantiated.

Then, a couple of months later, when John happened to be in
Boston, an ABAA dealer told him that Ken Anderson was offering
to sell a box of signed T. S. Eliots.

"Get them!" John said. "That way we can trace them back and
have some evidence."

But the dealer refused to buy books that might be worthless and
for which restitution was in no way guaranteed, so John returned to
San Francisco and sent a second e-mail on August 18.

SECURITY ADVISORY

Follow-up to the security committee's advisory about Ken
Anderson of Old Nail Books. . . . It has come to our attention
that Old Nail Books has recently offered a group of books by
T. S. Eliot, described as being signed or inscribed, to an ABAA
member. If any other member is contacted by Mr. Anderson,
please get in touch with the security committee, address below,
as soon as possible. And to those members who have had
contact with Old Nail Books in the past, it would be extremely
helpful to the security committee to have copies of any alleged
forgeries, if you can supply them.

This time, John got a response.

The year before, at the 1997 New York Antiquarian Book Fair,
Doug O'Dell of Chapel Hill Books of North Carolina had sold

four signed books to Tom Congalton of Between the Covers of New Jersey.

"It was two Eliots, and a Yeats . . . no, maybe three Eliots," said Doug. "They were very good. This guy just called me up one day. He said he had a bunch of books to sell. He was from Connecticut, and he told me that he was selling his father's books, that his father had been a collector and he had died. I said I would take a look at them and he sent me a bunch of books.

"I made him offers and some of them he accepted and some of them he said no, he could get more money elsewhere, so I sent those books back. One book, I remember, he said no to and then called me back a couple of days later and said he would take my of-fer after all.

"So, when I was at the '97 fair, I showed these four books to Tom and he bought them. About an hour later he came back. Tom had brought the books over to Peter Stern [of Peter L. Stern & Co., Boston]. Peter had taken one look at them and said, 'Did you hap-pen to buy these books from Ken Anderson?'"

"I had known about Anderson for years," said Peter Stern. "Some of his work was very good and some was awful. His Eliot was good, and so was his Yeats. His Hemingway wasn't bad either. But his Faulkner and Virginia Woolf were *terrible*. There were some books where there wasn't a single thing right about them. They should never have gotten past anyone."

The quality of the signatures was, and continues to be, a subject of ongoing debate. The consensus was that when Anderson first started, most of the signatures were easy to spot. His early Yeats, for example, was two or three times the size of a genuine Yeats signa-ture. And of course, the blind stamp soon became a dead giveaway, even if a potential buyer didn't know a thing about the signature. Also, the books in which these signatures were forged were always cheap editions—"scruffy," as one dealer described them; Anderson could have bought them for fifteen or twenty dollars. The value was solely in the signature. As time went on, however, Anderson got better: the blind stamp was gone, the quality of the signatures improved markedly—especially the Eliot and the Hemingway—and, most importantly, the books in which the signatures were forged were of a vastly higher quality and therefore tended to be handled by higher-end dealers, many of whom—for the first time—were ABAA members.

Doug O'Dell sent John the four books from the 1997 New York fair and other dealers sent books as well. When he had about ten or twelve books, John forwarded them to two experts in New York, James Lowe of James Lowe Autographs Ltd, and Chris Coover of Christie's.

Jim Lowe is a silver-haired man of about sixty who has been in the autograph business for over thirty years. His office is on 60th Street between Madison and Park, almost around the corner from Jim Cummins, with whom, along with four other dealers, he used to have an adjoining shop. "It was a great arrangement," Jim recalled. "It was Jim Cummins, myself, Margy Cohen, Ursus, and Harvey Tucker of Black Sun Books, all in the same place. We all wandered in and out of each other's shops, and compared books and signatures. Others have tried the idea since, but nobody made it work the way we did."

Jim Lowe's shop is a long narrow room with linoleum on the floor and a Formica desk and a round Formica table and four chairs. If the room itself is unremarkable, the decor is anything but. The walls are filled with dozens of framed autographed photographs of all sizes: Alexander Graham Bell, complete with white, bushy whiskers; Robert Morris with a bill of exchange; a letter by Claude Monet written in spidery purple ink; Arthur Rubinstein in profile with artistically long hair, Giuseppe Verdi, well-groomed, with a close-cropped beard; George Bernard Shaw looking over his glasses; and a stunning portrait of Sarah Bernhardt reclining on a couch in her famous swoon pose.

Jim Lowe has been an autograph collector for most of his life. "My first real experience was when I bought a book of love letters for twenty dollars—a *lot* of money to me then—and when I was looking through it, I found a letter from Charles Dickens tipped in.

"I really got my start at Mendoza's. It was the oldest antiquarian bookstore in New York—it was established before the turn of the century. They had a five-story building down on Ann Street, just north of the financial district. The first floor was open to the public, but the top four floors were where they did their cataloging and kept most of their stock. It was like Miss Havisham's in *Great Expectations*—dark, with a layer of dust on everything—but they had wonderful books.

"In any event, old man Mendoza had four sons and three of them went into the business. Each had a specialty—one did nineteenth-century literature, one did modern firsts, I forget what the third did. The fourth son was a playboy—he just wanted to fool around and have a good time. Of course, everybody died except the playboy and he ended up taking over the entire business. He was my friend. I went literally every day to the shop. We sat and talked for hours.

"When he died, the family wanted me to take over the business, but it wasn't for me. For one thing, Mendoza's didn't own the building and the landlord was going to increase the rent by an astronomical amount. Also, I wanted my own business—if I took over Mendoza's, I would be promoting their name, not mine."

Over the years, Jim has had more than his share of experience with forgers, especially the infamous John Jenkins, whom Jim described as "a short, loud, vulgar man—very intimidating. He walked around New York with these big cowboy hats and his briefcase had 'BULLSHIT' burnished into the leather. He treated women terribly.

"I got to know him quite well—unfortunately. There was an international conference here while he was president of the ABAA. He wanted a limousine to take him everywhere and, since I was the head of the planning committee, I was in the car with him all the time.

"John got power from his wealth—or what everyone thought was his wealth. You have to remember that back then the ABAA was still largely a gentleman's club. Many of the dealers were émigrés who had fled Europe just before World War Two. To them, book dealing was something you did after you were wealthy—as a hobby. It was very difficult to get in—only the recommendations of important dealers would get someone admitted. Not like today.

"John was vice president, then someone decided to put him up for president. They felt that he would bring in Texas. All the previous presidents had been from the East. What nobody knew was that John was very big into gambling. His wealth was illusionary—he owed huge sums of money. Although the standard story is that he committed suicide, most people in the trade think that he was murdered."

Jim didn't limit his acquaintances to murder victims—he dealt with murderers as well.

"Mark Hofmann was a customer of mine. He used to come on weekends and sit and talk for hours about philosophical or academic things. He made the rounds—Sotheby's, Christie's, Argosy, here. He was this short, owlish man—Casper Milquetoast—kind of round, always looked too big for his clothes. He studied my stock and sometimes bought photographs—unsigned, of course. Now I realize he was simply buying material to forge. He bought unsigned books from Argosy as well, then signed them and sold them to Sotheby's. Sometimes he even went to Sotheby's to watch his pieces sell.

"Hofmann was an excellent forger. He had definitely moved well out of just Mormon material. He had developed an extremely wide repertoire of what he could forge. He did Davy Crockett, Daniel Boone, and John Hancock. And he was very thorough. To get the right paper, he went to the big bins that Argosy used to keep outside their shop—where they threw away a lot of old material.

Hofmann dug out old books, tore out blank pages and, voilà, instant genuine nineteenth-century paper. He actually learned how to make ink from another autograph dealer. The dealer didn't know, of course, but Hofmann would sit around his shop on weekends, like he did at mine, and in the course of conversation ask questions like, 'Well, let's say someone wanted to make ink look like Davy Crockett's. How would they go about it?' and the dealer would say, 'Oh, you'd mix so much coffee grounds with water, then throw in a little oil. . . .' That kind of thing. I guess we were all helping Mark without realizing we were helping him.

"I never suspected Hofmann until the last weekend he came in here. He had four pieces. There was a van Gogh letter, one from Edgar Allan Poe, one from Benjamin Franklin, and something else. He wanted ninety thousand dollars. It was the first time in dealing with him that I thought something might be wrong. The paper didn't feel right—the grain wasn't in it. The ink was wrong too. I didn't want to take the pieces but I didn't want to look like I was accusing him of anything. I told him that I didn't think the letters were worth ninety thousand. He kept bargaining and lowering the price. It was clear that he was desperate for money. By the time he walked out of here, he was asking nine thousand dollars.

"The next week, he was arrested for murder."

Evidently, Kenneth Anderson's ploy of selling forged material at prices vastly lower than what would have been their actual value was not unique. "It has always been the forger's game," said Jim, "to sell too cheap."

Jim usually charges $250 per signature, but, as a member of the ABAA himself, he looked at the Anderson material for free.

"I knew instantly," he recalled. "The Eliots were competent forgeries but the wrong time period. I could see the Hemingways were wrong—in this business, you develop an instinct—but because I have such respect for John Crichton, I decided to do a little study."

To do his study, Jim placed a number of photostats of genuine Hemingway signature inscriptions from the 1920s on one sheet of paper, a number from the 1930s on a second, and those from the 1940s and 1950s on a third. He even had photostats of Hemingway's endorsements on the backs of checks. There, but never in books, he often signed "Ernest M. Hemingway."

"The forger is trying to create an illusion," said Jim, "so you look for things that don't fit. I noticed very quickly that, in the forgeries, the tails on the 'H' dip below the bottom of the other letters but in a genuine signature, they stop at the same level. Also, the second 'e' in Ernest should be strong and round, but in the forgeries, it is always thin and weak.

"On one of the books, John Crichton came up with the fact that Hemingway had not been in Sun Valley in 1945, when the inscription was dated. Forgers often don't do their research. There was once a Lincoln letter that sold at Sotheby's—a collector bought it for between one and two hundred thousand dollars. The collector came to me and asked to have the signature authenticated. It was a letter to John C. Frémont, asking him to come to dinner at the White House, to bring his wife—all very friendly. The only problem was that, on the day the letter was supposedly written, Frémont and his wife were in California and had been for three months. It was something Lincoln obviously would have known.

"That's what's so much fun about this business. Every problem is a little mystery and I get to play detective," said Jim.

The double-signed *Passages* did not present much of a problem at all. "This is very clumsy. Both signatures are obviously by the same person. The slant is wrong in both of them and so is the connection of letters. The Pound signature from this period should be larger than the Yeats. These forgeries are not even remotely competent."

After his examination, Jim quickly notified John Crichton of his findings.

Now, with evidence to back up the story, John, completely on his own, called "just about every bookseller in Connecticut and western Massachusetts." He discovered that Old Nail Books had begun to put out listing sheets and catalogs, trying to create the appearance of a legitimate dealer.

John now felt he had enough of a case to go to the authorities. He started in Anderson's hometown. Stafford Springs had only one police officer, and that person, by refusing to return telephone calls, effectively signaled that he had no interest in pursuing someone whose only crime appeared to be signing dead people's names in old books.

Having failed on the local level, John went for the big guns and called the FBI in San Francisco. They referred him to the FBI office in Connecticut, which, in turn, referred him to the FBI Web site. John dutifully sent a series of e-mails to the bureau describing Anderson's crime as "literary forgery." He waited but the FBI also, it seemed, had no interest. The same was to be true of the Connecticut attorney general's office, which, having received a similar e-mail, had given a similar nonreply.

Frustrated, John reread the content of the Connecticut attorney general's Web site and realized that, while the office might not appreciate the nuances of literary forgery, it was interested in "consumer fraud and counterfeiting." John then carefully reworked his e-mail and, on October 21, 1998, forwarded the following:

Dear Sir:
    I am writing to you in my capacity as Chairman of the Security Committee of the Antiquarian Booksellers' Association of America (ABAA). We have been looking into a very serious matter concerning counterfeiting, forgery and consequently consumer fraud which we have very good reason to believe is being perpetrated in the State of Connecticut. The victims, however, are spread out over various states. I have written a long letter to your office, with some documentation, and would like to know to whom I should direct such correspondence. As soon as I hear from you or your office, I will immediately send off the letter or, if you prefer, I can e-mail it.

Thank you, and I look forward to hearing from you.

Sincerely,
John Crichton

Although John Crichton was unaware of it, other ABAA dealers were becoming actively involved in the Kenneth Anderson case. John Wronoski of Lame Duck Books in Boston, for example, had recently sent an e-mail to some friends of his warning them about Anderson books.

"I'd been dealing with Anderson books for six or seven years," said John. "I deal a lot in association copies so I know what to look for. There were a lot of bad Anderson books so I had to send them back. For a long time, I didn't think it was Anderson himself who was doing it. I didn't think anyone would be that obvious. I just thought that he was getting bad books from someone else. Some of the other modern-first dealers like Waiting for Godot Books and Ken Lopez were getting some stuff too, so we talked about it and decided to try and warn people." John mentioned the name of another well-known, high-priced Boston dealer. "He was getting bad books too, but he didn't care.

"What I did was try and tell people who might have an Anderson book that they'd better check it. Remember, not all the books were bad, not even the signed ones. He sold a lot of signed books that were fine."

One of the people who received John's e-mail was Charles Agvent in Metztown, Pennsylvania, outside of Philadelphia.

"Just about the time Anderson started doing business as Old Nail," John went on, "I had seen some books in Charles Agvent's stock that seemed to be the same things that Anderson had offered to me, so I e-mailed him and told him to check."

Charles Agvent went the others one better and decided to engage in a little counterespionage.

"Anderson sent me three printed pages in late '97, January '98 at the latest," said Charles. "It was an Old Nail listing sheet. I didn't make the connection at first, and there were some books I was interested in, so I called him. He said that he had inherited the books from an uncle, maybe a grandfather, and that he needed money so he was selling them.

"I had never done business with him, so I said I needed to see the books first. He said that was fine and that he'd send them to me on approval. When I got the books, there was a lot of good stuff there—a signed Berryman, a signed Lowell—other books too. I agreed to buy some of them. I guess it was after I agreed to buy them but before I paid for them that I remembered John Wronoski's notice on-line. So, I only kept one book that I was absolutely sure was genuine and returned the Berryman and the Lowell.

"If it wasn't for the e-mail, I definitely would have kept them," Charles went on. "That's the thing about signatures—even if it's someone who you deal in all the time, you almost always have to have a signed book on hand to compare it to. With Eliot or Hemingway, that's not too difficult—there are so many signed copies around. But Berryman and Lowell—Berryman wrote in this cramped little hand—you need an example in front of you to match up.

"In any event, I had already put Anderson on my mailing list, which is what I do with everyone who sends me a catalog. In March, he called and told me he was interested in one of *my* books, a second edition of *The Wasteland,* without a dust jacket—unsigned of course. I gave him the twenty-percent dealer discount, which is what he had given me, and sold him the book for seven hundred and eighty dollars.

"I don't know why exactly, maybe it was instinct, but I decided to put my initials in the book. I wanted to see if the book would surface again. I went to a page almost at the end and wrote my initials very subtly, way down in the gutter."

In the meantime, two days after his revised counterfeiting and consumer fraud e-mail to the Connecticut attorney general's office, John got action. First, he received an e-mail:

Dear Mr. Crichton:
Thank you for your e-mail. I would suggest you direct your
letter to Valerie Bryan who is head of my Consumer Assistance
Unit. The address is Attorney General's Office, 110 Sherman
Street, Hartford, CT 06105.

Sincerely,
Richard Blumenthal
Attorney General

But before John could write to Valerie Bryan, she called him
and said that she was referring the matter to the state police. Two
days after that, Trooper Karen O'Connor of the Connecticut State
Police called and asked to arrange a meeting with John, herself, and
Special Agent Charles Urso of the FBI. Since this was just before
the Boston Antiquarian Book Fair in early November, for which
John would be coming east anyway, they were able to meet in Connecticut.

John took his ten or twelve suspicious Ken Anderson books,
the evidence from the autograph experts, and his story to Karen
O'Connor's office at the Connecticut State Police barracks in Nor-
wich, about an hour and a half from Boston.

"I GO FROM ZERO TO BITCH IN FIVE SECONDS," read
the sign on Trooper O'Connor's door.

John met with O'Connor and Urso for about forty-five minutes. Both were noncommittal. There was no question that a crime
had been committed; but what was going to happen next was prob-
lematic. In order to pursue the matter further, the FBI would have
to actively choose to proceed and there was no guarantee that they
would do so.

"It probably doesn't meet our level of dollars for fraud," Urso
warned John.

Charles Urso works out of a satellite FBI office in a three-story
concrete and glass building just off I-91 in Meriden, about fifteen
miles south of Hartford. There is a sales office of SNET on the

ground floor and the FBI shares the second floor with Dun & Bradstreet. Around the corner from the elevators is a plain single wooden door with the FBI seal on it. On the wall next to the door is a buzzer and an alarm keyboard that would be very formidable-looking except that the door isn't kept locked.

Inside is a small vestibule with a plate glass window (presumably bullet-proof) that looks out into a large open office. A walk-through metal detector stands just inside the door, but anyone can step around it with ease. On one wall is a small, framed photograph of the director, Louis Freeh, the kind of thing that could be replaced easily and cheaply in case Mr. Freeh is himself replaced, and on the other wall is a shabby framed poster called "Connecticut Architecture."

Next to the window is a red telephone with a little sign printed in script.

Attention Visitors
Please use the red telephone to contact a
secretary regarding your visit to the FBI
Thank you

Special Agent Charles Urso was in his forties, tall and heavy, with brown hair. He was wearing an open-necked, long-sleeve, button-down, brown and red plaid shirt, light brown corduroys, and no gun. He was open and affable, with a warm smile and a twinkle in his eye, much more a person you'd meet at a new neighbor's barbecue than a hard-as-nails G-man gunning down Baby Face Nelson. When he introduced himself, he stuck out his hand and said, "Hi. I'm Charlie."

Charlie got the Anderson case on a referral. "It came in on a day that it was my duty, like today. I had to handle citizen complaints, anyone who calls in. Karen O'Connor from the state police called. She told me about the case and asked me if I was interested.

"You have to understand—Connecticut is unique in that the state police don't have subpoena power. All they can do is get a search warrant and turn a suspect's office or residence inside out. But if a suspect has a dummy residence or keeps records in a car with something that could be exculpatory, a smart lawyer can use the whole thing to help build a defense. The state police can't compel a suspect to produce financial records or other materials, so anything with an economic impact, they come to us.

"After I told Karen we'd look into it, I ran it around the department and said, 'Hey, anyone want this?' Everyone said, 'Nah.' It's like the military here. You do what you're given but you don't like to volunteer.

"I usually handle business cases—large-scale fraud or public corruption. I have an M.B.A. and I've been doing this for twenty-one years. When I went over the details, I thought, 'Hey, this might be fun.' We don't get to work with the state police that often and it was in an area I don't know much about. So I kept the case myself. I squeezed it in. Now I have an art case too. Twenty-one years and suddenly I have two of these kind of cases.

"I saw right away that most of the work had already been done. The book industry people had gotten together a pretty solid body of evidence so we were just piggybacking on the industry case. They would have made very good investigators."

After meeting with the FBI and the Connecticut State Police, John headed for the Boston Antiquarian Book Fair. The Boston fair, while not attracting quite the same level of attendance as the New York fair, is nonetheless one of the premier ABAA events. In addition to every important dealer in the East, the Boston fair gets more than its share of West Coast and international representation.

Originally, John had intended to take advantage of the Boston fair to warn the members about the Anderson forgeries by distributing the following broadside:

Lawrence and Nancy Goldstone

BEWARE!
A FORGER

THE SIGNATURES AND INSCRIPTIONS BELOW ARE FORGERIES! which have been perpetrated in the recent past by one or more forgers thought to be operating in the New England area. These forgeries are being widely circulated throughout the antiquarian book trade. In addition to the examples below, the forger is known to be counterfeiting the signatures and/or inscriptions of John Steinbeck, William Faulkner, Rudyard Kipling, Evelyn Waugh, Joseph Conrad, Thomas Hardy and Ezra Pound. And there are certainly others as yet undetected or unreported.

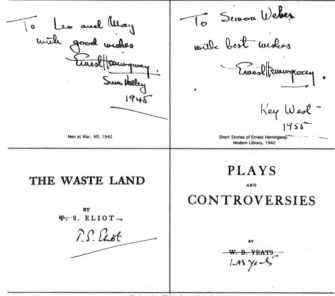

(Reduced to 75% of actual size)

The members of Antiquarian Booksellers' Association of America want the public, other members of the trade and librarians to be able to purchase with confidence any signed or inscribed book. The ABAA is committed to a strict Code of Ethics, and it members unconditionally guarantee the authenticity of all materials sold by them. To this end, we will endeavor to expose and rid the marketplace of bogus material, such as the examples above. Anyone with information which might lead to the identity and possible prosecution of this forger or forgers is encouraged to contact the Security Committee of the ABAA. <abaasecurity@brickrow.com>.

The Antiquarian Booksellers' Association of America
20 West 44th St., New York, NY 10036. (212) 944-8291; Fax: (212) 944-8293

At the last minute, however, he decided against a formal announcement. Although he had still heard nothing official, the state police and FBI might very possibly be investigating Anderson, and John didn't want to do anything to jeopardize the case.

But even without police notification, the Boston Book Fair was to yield up a key piece of evidence.

During the first day, when dealers do a lot of walking around and checking out what the others have brought, Charles Agvent happened to stop by the booth rented by Bauman Rare Books. Bauman's is top-of-the-line in terms of both quality and price. They have a shop on Madison Avenue and regularly take out full-page ads in the *New York Times Book Review* advertising things like first editions of *Ulysses* or *Alice in Wonderland*. Bauman's is owned by David Bauman and his wife, Natalie.

"I was speaking with Natalie," said Charles Agvent, "and she happened to mention that she had bought an inscribed copy of *The Wasteland*."

Charles was immediately curious and asked Natalie which edition it was. When she said it was a second, he asked to see it. But Bauman's had just gotten the book in, and had yet to price it, and therefore had not brought it to the fair.

"So I told her about the book I had sold to Anderson," said Charles. "Natalie called her shop right away and told them to check the page I told her about. When they did, they found my initials."

Without saying anything to John Crichton, Charlie Urso and Karen O'Connor had indeed decided to take a shot at Anderson.

"When Karen and I first went out to his place, we didn't know what to expect," said Charlie. "Old Nail Books might have been a big office with ten employees. You know, maybe this guy had moved to Stafford Springs to be out in the country and bought himself ten acres and a big house. But as soon as we saw that Anderson lived in a tiny garden apartment, we knew we had a slam-dunk.

"We went by twice but there wasn't anyone home. We didn't want to leave a card or a note asking him to call the office. We wanted to hit him cold. He was operating as a company so he didn't have Fifth Amendment privileges. When we went by the third time, there wasn't anyone there either—this was starting to take up a lot of time. Then we saw his car pull in. Karen had done the background on him and knew the car.

"So we got out and we identified ourselves. We said, 'We have some complaints that some of the product offered from Old Nail Books isn't what it's supposed to be.' You want to be general. You don't want him to know exactly what you know.

"He started giving ambiguous answers, like 'I'm not sure what you mean.' Then he started talking about books and covers, and five hundred thread weaves or something. Basically, he was babbling and scared shitless. You know, he was totally lying, displaying all the behavior of a person guilty of this. His comfort level was talking about the books and we didn't want to talk about the books. Then, after about half an hour of books and covers and God knows what else, I thought, 'Okay, he's not going to give it up today.' And then Karen hit him.

"I'm very low-key when I'm interviewing someone—kind of the way I am now. Karen came in and said, 'Kenneth, now's the time to show cooperation, when you're first confronted.'

"Then he totally gave it up. We went into his apartment—it was a zoo in there—and looked through his records and found what we needed to complete the case.

"We had him," said Charlie. "It didn't matter at that point if he denied it or even if he had destroyed his records. What was he going to do, say that he dealt in these two-and-three-thousand-dollar books but he didn't remember where he got them? 'I bought them from some guy on the street'? If you were a juror, would you believe that? He has to have *something* to authenticate his purchases. We have to have enough to go into court and prove his guilt beyond a reasonable doubt. Between what the book people had done and what Karen came up with, we had more than enough. No—one way he was screwed, the other he was creamed.

"So we memorialized what he said in a statement—basically, that he's admitted to his responsibility. I told him to call the public defender's office—it was clear he didn't have the money for his own attorney—to help him protect his rights. The PD's office did a good job. They worked out a deal with the U.S. attorney's office. This was a unique situation because Kenneth had inventory for restitution."

On March 18, 1999, Kenneth Russell Anderson pled guilty to one count of felony mail fraud in Federal District Court in New Haven, Connecticut. As part of his plea agreement, Anderson agreed to make full restitution to all those he had defrauded.

The plea agreement cites the sale of forty-five books to seventeen dealers in twelve states, for which, according to the purchasing dealers, Anderson received $33,000. Ultimately, there were fifty-six books on the list, valued at $36,570, but the U.S. attorney allowed the $33,000 number to stand. In every case the buyer was an **ABAA** member, and the roster is something of a Who's Who. Among the names are Heritage Books, Jim Cummins, George Minkoff, Kevin MacDonnell, Bauman Rare Books, Glen Horowitz, and Thomas Dorn.

"Full restitution to all those he had defrauded," however, is a somewhat smokier concept than it might first appear. Anderson only admitted to having begun his activities in early 1998, and the plea agreement was under a federal charge that was tied to his doing business as Old Nail Books. That left a lot of territory uncovered.

But much more importantly, there was the question of whether other dealers would come forward. Certainly, anyone who still had an Old Nail book in inventory would turn it in and get their money back. But what about a book that had already been resold? Restitution was only for the price that the victimized dealer paid Old Nail. Anderson was notorious for selling his forged work at prices vastly under market value. That meant that a dealer's resale price might have garnered a substantial profit, in some cases in excess of five thousand dollars, possibly even more. Would that dealer now contact his customer, admit that he or she had unwittingly bought and then sold a forgery, and then refund the customer's money, all to turn in a book for which the dealer would recoup perhaps ten cents on the dollar, and not even that if Anderson was broke?

Some did. Jim Cummings had sold an inscribed Hemingway to his best customer, a collector in the UK. "It was a nondescript book," said Jim, "but it was inscribed to someone plausible. I didn't know until the '98 New York fair. Even then, I didn't know for sure, but I knew it was an Anderson book, so I got it back. My customer and I laugh about it now, but I didn't then."

"Jim Cummins sweated blood about getting in touch with his customer and getting the book back," Terry Halladay told us. "It's the worst thing a bookseller can ever have to do. But Jim did it."

But where some dealers like Jim, or John Crichton, or Terry Halladay, would do anything to maintain the integrity of their industry, for others, the temptation to keep their mouths shut must have been powerful indeed. There was certainly little enough risk in doing so. They knew that Anderson wasn't about to admit to forging any more books than he had to.

Anderson had agreed that any books in his personal collection might be sold in order to help satisfy the thirty-three-thousand-dollar judgment against him. In March, a small contingent met at Anderson's apartment.

"So then," said Charlie Urso, "the funniest thing that happened in the whole case was when we went to his house to evaluate his books. I wanted the PD, the public defender, to come along to see the place—because, you know, there was no way to describe it to a person. All those books and the cats crawling up the sofa. So there we were, me, Karen, John, and another book guy, and the PD. Kenneth was there with his girlfriend and we're all trying to squeeze into this tiny apartment."

"John had called me because I was from the area and knew something about modern firsts," said Peter Stern. "When we went to Anderson's apartment to evaluate the books that he was putting up for restitution, the state policewoman looked around and said, 'Usually, I deal in bloodstains, not ink stains.'"

"Then we go in," said Charlie, "and he's got a dozen doughnuts and the coffee on, and it was like he was trying to make it into this Greenwich Village reading thing. Kenneth wanted to make it like a real-time event, you know it was the social opportunity of the year for him, it was a time for him to talk to the experts about what he loved best."

"It was kind of pathetic, really," said Peter Stern. "Here we were coming to take anything he had of value to make up for a felony, and he wants to talk about books. He knows what he's talking about too. He knows about books."

"I finally met the guy in March with Peter Stern," said John Crichton. "He's not so intimidating in person. He was a quick study, though. He'd obviously read a lot of biographies and book-collecting books—he'd grown almost logarithmically in his ability to adapt to the trade and its nuances. He was a very smart guy."

"The book guys, they weren't having any of it," said Charlie. "This was like a jihad for them. Kenneth wanted to bring out each book and talk about it, but they knew what they were doing and didn't need him. It only took them about an hour and a half. All they cared about was if there was going to be enough to do a tag sale."

"While we were going through the books," said Peter, "Charlie Urso mentioned that he had just bought some sports memorabilia—a couple of things signed by Joe DiMaggio. You know, DiMaggio had just died. Suddenly, he looked up and said, 'Hey, Ken, you didn't do Joe DiMaggio, did you?'"

"I didn't want to engage him in conversation," said John. "I was aggravated at him. But the police didn't want him to talk to us anyway. There was more to it than money. There's something very sad about it. He regularly ordered other books from booksellers off the Internet and catalogs. He even put out a couple of catalogs of his own. He might have someday been a good bookseller."

"Nobody ate any of the doughnuts," noted Peter Stern.

The lead story in the spring 1999 issue of the ABAA newsletter was John Crichton's account of his pursuit of Kenneth Anderson, entitled "New England Forger Brought to Justice." The article was accompanied by a photograph of John piloting a dogsled in some snow-covered wilderness. The caption read, "ABAA Security Committee Chair John Crichton, in dogged pursuit of stolen books and forgers, seen here searching the wilds of the Canadian border."

"I took my step-daughter dogsledding in Minnesota," John explained, a little bashfully.

Considering that he had more or less single-handedly pursued and apprehended a person who was preying on his industry, Crichton's article is remarkably free of self-aggrandizement. But there is no masking the anger that John felt toward Kenneth Anderson. He referred to him in the article as "a twenty-eight-year-old want-to-be bibliophile," and "a textbook confidence man."

He further wrote:

> Anderson quickly learned from his mistakes and diligently worked at perfecting his craft. Soon the embossed stamp was gone, the list of forged authors expanded, and the forgeries were more skillfully executed. Association copies began appearing. Several of these offered a carefully constructed bogus provenance in the form of older booksellers' descriptions laid in. About two years ago, Anderson began doing business as the Old Nail Shop and issued the

first of his catalogs. His choice of business name was a perverse act of flaunting his crime: rust from old nails was widely used in the nineteenth century to cause paint pigments in forged master paintings to appear older than they were. Clearly confident and brazen, Anderson expanded his operation by directly quoting books to booksellers outside of Connecticut. Word had not yet spread out of central New England about this potential forger, and few booksellers were aware of his new, improved efforts.

In closing, John noted: "He is [now] only 32 years old and deceptively crafty. Let's cross our fingers and hope he forever leaves us alone, but don't count on it."

On June 22, 1999, all the material that Kenneth Anderson had offered for restitution was put up at auction at Oinonen Book Auctions in Sunderland, Massachusetts. There were over five hundred books, manuscripts, photographs, and pamphlets condensed into 125 lots. Although there were some unusual items, the books were, by and large, first trade editions of newer works, with a heavy emphasis on poetry.

There were two books from Cuala Press, both by Yeats—a first edition, second printing, of *On the Boiler* and *A Packet for Ezra Pound,* one of a limited run of 425. Both were blind-stamped. Neither was inscribed. It made Terry Halladay's thesis about the razored page of the double-signed *Letters of John Butler Yeats* all the more interesting. It is certainly possible that Anderson had begun to raid his own library for books in which to forge signatures but knew enough by this time to get rid of the blind stamp, even at the expense of suppressing the value. It is also possible that Anderson sold the book with the blind stamp and somewhere along the line one of the dealers through whose hands the books passed got rid of the Anderson stigma on his or her own.

There was, in fact, only one book in the entire collection that did not have the Anderson blind stamp. That book was a 1922 Paris edition of *Ulysses,* one of 750 numbered copies on handmade paper. It had been rebound in modern cloth-backed boards. At a valuation between $1,000 and $2,000, it was easily the most valuable book in the entire auction.

"Every book except the *Ulysses* was blind-stamped," said Peter Stern. "It makes you wonder, doesn't it?"

Peter had originally estimated that everything together might fetch as much as $20,000. That would, of course, go a long way toward satisfying the $33,000 obligation to which Anderson had agreed. In fact, the auction only realized $14,717, and that included $3,900 for the *Ulysses.*

"There was just no interest," Dick Oinonen went on. "A lot of dealers stayed away. Nobody said anything to me, but I have a feeling that they had kind of agreed to an unofficial boycott. I think they felt, 'We're not going to do anything to help that SOB.'"

"There wasn't a boycott," said Terry Halladay. "At least nothing that I knew about. But these were damaged goods, and with the blind stamp they were damaged physically as well as morally."

"I guess something went wrong," said Charlie Urso, "because they didn't make as much as they thought they were going to. But I guess it's not such a bad thing that Kenneth is going to have to work for a few years to make up the difference."

A sentencing hearing in *United States of America vs. Kenneth R. Anderson* was held on June 29, 1999, in United States District Court in Hartford, Connecticut. Although the presiding judge, Janet Bond Arterton, had a good deal of leeway, the probation report and federal sentencing guidelines had already more or less determined Anderson's punishment. The preliminary sentence was to include three years' probation, the first six months of which would be voice-monitored house arrest; three hundred hours of community service; psychological counseling; and the $33,000 restitution, less the $14,717 realized at the auction. Unless Anderson completely blew it at the hearing, he would spend no time at all in prison.

"I never met him," said Terry Halladay. "I only saw him at his sentencing hearing. He was sitting out in the hall complaining how the article in the ABAA newsletter was unfair in portraying him as an archcriminal. He was quite vehement about it, which I found very irritating. I thought, if it was me who was getting off lightly—house arrest, after all—I would just be sitting there with my mouth shut, grateful that I wasn't going to jail."

By the time Anderson addressed the court, however, his vehemence had apparently cooled.

I am aware that the crime I committed really has much more far reaching consequences than the legal consequences. There are ethical consequences and the question of trust. This is one of the last businesses where a person can get by with a handshake and a promise, where they will not take a credit card, Your Honor, but will take a personal check. It's a business built on trust, and that is something that I violated. More than the imposition of restitution, fines, sentencing, there is a deep and abiding shame in me that I will carry for a very long time, probably for good, as regards to the thing I've done. . . .

I have taken every avenue, pursued every route open to me to make some kind of restitution, to make some kind of amends for this, and I sincerely intend to make full restitution to the people that I've wronged in the hope that that gesture may restore some sense of at least justice, if not trust, between myself and those people that I've wronged, which doesn't just stop at dealers, but the individual people with whom the dealers work and sell to on a daily basis. It hurts me very much.

Although Judge Arterton replied, "It probably would not surprise you to know that a great many people standing in your position before the Court at the time of sentencing express a deep sense of shame, remorse, and so forth," she allowed the preliminary sentence to stand, and Kenneth Anderson left the courtroom to begin his six months of house arrest.

And so, the bad guy got caught, the good guys did the catching, and the victims will someday get at least most of their money back.

That closed out the Ken Anderson story. Or did it?

Stafford Springs, settled in 1719, is in northeast Connecticut, about four miles off I-84, an interstate connecting New York and Boston by way of Hartford. You get off at Exit 70 and then head north on Route 32, past towering fir trees and the Rainbow Acres campground, until you get to the center of town, which is marked by a fountain leading to the spring that gave the town its name. The fountain was demolished by a semi-truck some years ago, but has recently been repaired using contributions from local citizens.

The center of town is about two blocks long. To the left of the fountain is the Stafford Springs Congregational Church, an old stone faux-medieval building complete with clock tower. Across the street is the Stafford Historical Society, a low, red-brick, one-story building that, in a former life, might have been a train station. On this same street can be found, in order, Molly Malone Fish & Chips (Take-Out Only), the Ice Cream Depot (Now Proudly Serving U Conn Ice Cream), and Scott's Collectibles (Non-sports, Sports, Racing, and Magic Cards). The number of viable businesses dwindles as you head away from the fountain, and by the second block the number of empty storefronts exceeds those of working retail establishments by two to one.

"*Deliverance* country," as one of the law enforcement officials involved in the case put it.

Ken Anderson lived in a dark, airless one-bedroom apartment

in the center of a six-unit garden apartment building. There was a small narrow efficiency kitchen off the living room. Bookshelves were everywhere. A couple were full, but most were bare, stripped of those five hundred books that had been auctioned off at Oinonen's. There were more bookcases in the bedroom and those were also sparsely stocked. On the walls were neatly framed autographed letters and photographs, mostly from poets like Stephen Spender, James Merrill, and John Ashbery, all a result of Anderson's personal correspondence. There was one cat, which seemed reasonably well behaved, and, given what there was to work with, the apartment showed taste and a definite esthetic sensibility.

Anderson, who looked even younger than thirty-two, had longish brown hair and a neat beard. He was heavy and wore wire-rimmed glasses, an open-necked, red, short-sleeved shirt, and black slacks. He grew up in nearby South Windsor, a suburb of Hartford. His grandfather was a stair-builder and his father was a contractor whose business, Valley Pine Company, failed in 1991. He had one sibling, a brother, who, like the rest of the family, went into lumber.

"It was always expected that I would go into the business," said Anderson, although a less likely candidate for the building trades would have been hard to find, something of which Anderson seemed all too aware.

"I had a difficult time reading at first—in elementary school I remember I had a sticker on my desk so that I could distinguish *d*s from *b*s—but in high school I really started devouring books. My teachers would say, 'Try this.' Or, 'If you liked that, try this one.'"

He went to the University of Connecticut at Storrs about twenty miles from home and majored in English literature. "I liked the library," he said. "I had a teacher, J. D. O'Hara, who taught me how to write a sentence without fumbling. He gave me some very good advice. He said, 'Always assume that the reader is slightly more intelligent than you are—less knowledgeable, but more intelligent.'

"By this time, I was trying to find the cheapest source for my reading. At first, that meant paperbacks of old books. But you know, they're so badly bound, they fall apart. I started to say to myself, 'If I can just find a cheap source of books that are better bound.' So I looked in the phone book and started visiting the used-book stores and discovered that I could get a good hardcover book for less than a paperbook."

Used-book stores provided social opportunities as well.

"I knew Ken when he was a student at U Conn," John Gambino, owner of Coventry Books in Coventry, Connecticut, said later. "That was more than ten years ago. He used to come into my shop all the time. He never bought a book—he spent hours going through them but never bought anything. He came in to talk. Usually he wanted to talk about Eliot or Pound. One time he put up a notice for a literature club he was organizing. At one point, he stopped coming in. I guess he had left school."

"I got into first editions by accident," Anderson continued. "While I was in college, there was a great resurgence of T. S. Eliot and an article appeared in the *New Yorker*—I think it was by Cynthia Ozick. She had excerpted Eliot and basically called him an anti-Semite. I wanted to read the whole passage—I don't like excerpts—but nobody had the book. I looked and looked, and finally I found it, but it was a first edition. I'm like, 'Why is this book so expensive?' It turned out that the book had an interesting story. When it first came out, Eliot said he was in a disturbed state of mind when he wrote it. There were no reprints and he tried to suppress it. According to Stephen Spender, he wouldn't even sign it. So I spent the fifty dollars, which was a struggle in college. I saved up over a month or two. Of course, no one else was beating down the door to buy the book.

"That was the start of it—all these books have a story. Then I started wondering how many first editions I had, and it turned out that I had bought some by chance. From there, I moved to associations. If Pound had helped Eliot to write *The Wasteland,* I'd better read some Pound. That's how my books are stacked—in the order of association."

Anderson has tried writing poetry in addition to reading it. "I've had some poems published in small literary magazines—*Hermes Crossing* and *Ironwood* out of Iowa. My family left me alone about it—I mean, they certainly didn't discourage me. My mother cautiously encouraged me but she told me, 'It will probably be a dead end.'"

He also began to correspond with several poets. "I met Jim Merrill—I accosted him in a restaurant," said Anderson. "I was with my parents, and I left them and went over to him and said, 'You're James Merrill, I recognize you from the back of your books, I love your work.' And he was so gracious. Afterwards, I wrote him a letter asking him to recommend where I could find a certain book of his and then, four days before my birthday, a package arrived—he had sent it to me, the *New Selected Poems*. He was terrific, a terrific poet, so generous. I said, 'I'd really like a copy of your book,' but he said, 'No, don't buy it, it's terrible.' So, out of respect for him I never read it."

Anderson pointed to a copy of *Ulysses* on his shelf. It was a newer trade edition. "I don't like that edition," he said. "It has the revised text. In the original, Joyce wrote, 'What is the word known to all men?' and the mother dies without answering the question. But after Joyce was dead, they dug up his notes, and Germans being Germans, they wanted to fit everything in, so they have the mother answer, 'love.'" He paused. "It caused a big stink when it came out. A lot of Joycean scholars went crazy."

As he was speaking, the telephone rang. "That must be the verification system," he said. He excused himself and answered the telephone. He paused, and then said his name. Then he paused again and said a short phrase. After three of these, he hung up.

"I'm the first person in the state to get home confinement," he said. "It's all done by computerized telephone calls. When I pick up the phone, it says, 'This is the containment verification system. This call is for Kenneth Anderson.' Then there's, 'Sit up straight. Don't have anything in your mouth. Don't use strange voices. Speak in your normal voice. Repeat after me.' Then the machine gives out some phrases—I'm not supposed to say what they are. The order is random. I repeat each one, then the machine thanks me and hangs up."

Anderson's book buying had become so pervasive that, in 1996, he got himself a tax number, so, according to him, "I could get the dealer discount," an automatic 20 percent off the price of any book purchased from another dealer. Although he is hazy about it, it is around this time that he seems to have started doing business as Old Nail Books, selling only to other dealers.

"I got the name 'Old Nail' from the Old Nail Bookshop that Robert Frost frequented when he was in England," Anderson recalled. "I remember my girlfriend thought it was perfect, both because of the Frost connection and because my family was in lumber and contracting. John Crichton, in his ABAA article, called it a thumb in the eye of the book community, that old nails were used for carbon deposits in art forgeries and that I was brazenly announcing myself as a forger, but that wasn't it at all. I was very hurt by that article and that assumption.

"For a while the business went okay," said Anderson. "My family was proud of me. And then, at the tail end of 1996 everything came to a screeching halt—an event happened, not something that I can talk about, but the result was that I didn't get out to get the books and the business was neglected. So early in 1997 . . . I started doing it. I wasn't enjoying it; I was looking for a way to get enough money to live on. I always lived on the money for as long as possible before doing it again. I just didn't want to have to leave for long periods to find books."

Not surprisingly, there are many who dispute Anderson's chronology.

"One day, maybe five years ago [in 1994]," John Gambino recalled, "out of the blue, he came in again but this time he wanted to sell me some books. A lot of them were signed. He had bills of sale; some of them were very elaborate. He had one from [an important dealer in western Massachusetts] for a book that he had bought for six or seven hundred dollars that he was willing to sell for three hundred. He said he had been collecting but that his family had run into financial difficulty and he had to sell.

"I looked at the books and asked him right away why he was coming to me. I was sure he could have sold them for a lot more in Boston or New York. He told me that other dealers didn't like that the books were blind-stamped.

"I bought a lot of the books and resold them to other dealers. There was one book that came back bad but it was only ten dollars. In another one, there was a question about the signature so I asked Ken where he got it. He said that he had bought some of the books from a man in Florida, and that he didn't know but some of them might not be good."

"As far as I know, I was the first person he came in to sell books to," said Bob Willig of Troubadour Books in North Hatfield, Massachusetts. "It was in October 1995. He was erudite, and very knowledgeable about books, especially literature and poetry. He said something about an uncle who had been a literary secretary to someone or other and had a good collection. He came into my shop and said he had some books he thought I would like.

"They were a mixture of signed and unsigned books. He had some first-edition Eliots and a signed Conrad, I remember. It was funny, because when I asked him about the other first-edition dealers in the area, Ken Lopez and Waiting for Godot Books . . . he didn't seem to know any of them."

One thing everyone agrees on, even Anderson, was that his first attempts were clumsy. "I don't know what the hell I was thinking of," said Anderson. "I had blind-stamped my books starting in high school, even the paperbacks. I guess even writing your name in a book is somehow establishing dominion. Even if you give them up, they are out there somewhere, marked as yours."

The reason for the blind-stamping, Anderson claims, is that he was raiding his own collection to raise money. "The books were here and I knew they would be more valuable with the signatures," he said.

Amateurish as it might have seemed, the blind-stamping at first worked in Anderson's favor with some dealers.

"I liked him," said Bob Willig, "but even from the beginning it felt like something was wrong. There was never really anything you could put your finger on, though. Then when I saw that most of the books were blind-stamped, I thought, who would blind-stamp a book that was bad?"

Even in this early period, Anderson's activities seemed to have been more extensive than he indicated, although at first he stayed away from the more sophisticated dealers, who might be quicker to spot a bad signature.

"Oh, it's been years," said a midrange dealer in central Massachusetts. "But it was pretty much of a local phenomenon in the Pioneer Valley [around Northampton]. This guy was coming into a lot of shops—not here—with signed books. I remember a lot of T. S. Eliot. He told people that he had inherited a collection. But they were never good books—rare, I mean. The books themselves were always fairly common—ten-or-fifteen-dollar books, even if they were firsts. The value was all in the signatures. And then he'd sell them signed for way, way under their value. Sometimes he sold books worth hundreds for twenty-five or thirty dollars.

"Some of the early stuff was pretty bad. He used a ballpoint pen a couple of times. Then, the other thing . . . the blind-stamping. When I first saw his books, a couple of other dealers had brought them in, I saw right away that they didn't look right. There was a Robert Lowell, I remember . . . certain authors sign in certain places and have certain characteristics. When the word started getting around, a lot of people didn't want to believe it. I remember one dealer telling me that he was thinking of buying a box of books from Ken Anderson and I told him not to. He yelled at me and told me I didn't know what I was talking about."

"The reason people around here first started getting suspicious," said Bob Willig, "was that it seemed like he had an endless supply of good books. So people started wondering whether he was stealing books, that maybe the uncle story was true in its basis but he was adding to it. A couple of people speculated that maybe he was forging books, but nobody knew anything for sure. Also, he really knew his stuff. And he had balls. He would strike up a legitimate correspondence with people like John Ashbery and Stephen Spender and walk in with a big handful of letters. So, when he walked into the shop with a signed Elizabeth Bishop, you said to yourself, well, she did speak at U Conn, and he does approach people." (This seems to be stretching a point since Elizabeth Bishop died in 1979, when Anderson was twelve.)

Nonetheless, after a while, most of the dealers in Massachusetts and Connecticut knew that books that came from Ken Anderson were, at the very least, suspicious. Many refused to buy books from him and some banned him from their shops entirely.

"We passed the word around as best we could," said the mid-range dealer, "but there's really no formal mechanism for disseminating this sort of thing. We're not ABAA."

But even as the small network of regional used-book dealers that he had been using began to be closed off to him, Anderson was already taking things to the next level.

"He started branching out," said Bob Willig, "and selling books to the heavy hitters, like Buddenbrooks and Heritage. So a lot of people around here said, 'Well, if *they* don't think anything's wrong . . .'"

"There were hundreds of books, maybe thousands," said another dealer, who also was not in the ABAA. "What's more, a lot of the dealers had to know what they were buying. There's one story about [a New England ABAA dealer] who drove out to Anderson's house because Anderson had told him this was the first time he had sold any books and as he drove up, he saw [another New England ABAA dealer] walking out of Anderson's apartment to his car with a box load of books."

"When he started putting out catalogs, that really confused people," Bob Willig went on. "After all, if you're doing something crooked, you'd quietly sell a five-hundred-dollar book to a dealer. You wouldn't put out a catalog and publicize what you're doing. And he was really smart about some books, too. There was a book called *Nine O'Clock High Stories* that he bought from me for two hundred dollars—he had started buying better books—and he put it into his catalog for six hundred because he noticed that a British dealer was offering it for six-fifty. And there was nothing wrong with that book."

It was during this period that the blind stamp disappeared and some (although not all) of the signatures began to improve. But in response to the assertion that he got better at forging over time, Anderson guffawed.

"I don't think the signatures got any better—they are all clumsy as hell, embarrassingly painful, really. They [the other dealers] think I had this plot. But if they couldn't tell the provenance at a glance, they are just making excuses. I never saw a signed Yeats—I used the embossed monogram on the front of the book as a model—I mean, the signatures were really crude stuff. I don't remember exactly how I came to do the Hemingway stuff."

Despite Anderson's denials, by the time of the sale to Chapel Hill Books in 1997, he had become sufficiently accomplished, at least in Eliot and Hemingway, that a reputable dealer like Doug O'Dell, who hadn't been warned, could be legitimately fooled. But what of the long period between the clumsy early work and the high-quality forgeries sold to Doug, the first time an ABAA member owned up to dealing with him? To whom was Ken Anderson selling his books?

"I was dumbfounded at the '98 fair to find out that (a) he was still selling books, and (b) he was selling quite widely," said Terry Halladay. "I thought he had dried up.

"I had seen some of his work earlier in connection with something else. A library had asked me to authenticate another Yeats signature on a book they'd gotten from Anderson. It was an obvious forgery. The signature was three or four times larger than a genuine Yeats."

Apparently, Ken Anderson had never dried up at all. If anything, he had been steadily escalating his activities. If not, how else was he getting the money to go from $10 and $15 books to $700 and $800 books? But if some of those early forgeries—like the oversized Yeats—were so poor, how was it that the more sophisticated dealers with whom he had obviously begun to do business had failed to spot them?

"If they didn't know, they should have," said Terry.

Once Anderson had successfully moved to the big time, he began to think of himself as something of a literary Robin Hood. "I only sold to dealers who could afford it," he said. "And I gave them every opportunity to know a book was bad. I often said, 'I'm not sure about this book. I think you should check it out.'"

In this, astoundingly, Anderson may have been telling the truth. A number of dealers, Charles Agvent and Doug O'Dell included, have said that Anderson was more than happy to send books on approval, and that he never complained when a dealer had the slightest reservation about authenticity. This may have been because Anderson knew that there was always another dealer out there willing to take it off his hands.

"You'd be surprised how many dealers never questioned anything," Anderson said. "There was one book that [a major dealer] was going to sell as a first and I said, 'No, no. It's a second.' I even told them where to check a bibliography. Then, when I got their catalog, I saw they were still calling it a first."

According to Anderson, it was only a fluke of timing that got him caught. "When I stopped—which was the summer of 1998, I stopped myself. But I stopped with the book they used as ironclad proof. They said, 'Let's get this guy.'"

The book they "got" him with was, of course, the second edition of *The Wasteland* that he had bought unsigned from Charles

Agvent and sold inscribed to Bauman's. By that time, "I could smell them on to me," said Anderson. "Usually, if I had bad material—dummied stuff or stuff I knew was dummied—I picked a dealer who I thought could absorb the damage. The ones with the big bucks. I'd call up and say 'I have this item, caveat caveat emptor. I don't know the source, I want you to verify it.' For me, at my end, I got raped over with the good stuff. When you say, 'I have a Steinbeck or a Kipling, but I'm not sure about the source,' you run it through your head. If you think it's worth nine hundred, you immediately cut it in half, so you're right away at four-fifty. Then you have to take the twenty percent dealer discount off, so now you're at three-fifty. Sometimes I would hear, 'Three-fifty is too high.' But when they were on to me, people would just say, 'Thanks, no thanks, we pass this time.' The tone of the conversation would change, like I was selling diseased meat.

"The rumors started instantly. This is a tiny world, they know instantly when something's wrong," said Anderson.

According to Anderson, he ended up selling *The Wasteland* with the forged signature to Bauman for eight hundred dollars. "I started at fifteen hundred but they beat me down," he explained. (The restitution sheet listed the book as being sold for twelve hundred dollars, an amount for which both Bauman's and John Crichton insist there is written documentation.)

"I had bought that book for myself," Anderson went on, "it was something I did for myself. I didn't intend to use it. I had to give up something I really wanted to keep. And then, in December, bang. I got the knock on the door and the FBI were in for lunch."

When asked what his long-term aspirations were, Anderson said, "To be a legitimate member of the community. The worst thing about all of this is that I'll never be able to have anything to do with the book business again. I wish more than anything that I could get John Crichton not to hate me. I knew what I was doing was wrong and dangerous, but I was hoping I could stop it before the business was ruined. That's why I almost never advertised any bad material in my catalogs."

Once again, a number of dealers take issue with this statement.

"That isn't right," Charles Agvent said. "I bought a Lowell from his catalog that was bad. It was smart of him to mix some bad things in with a lot of good. I don't think it had anything to do with his wanting to keep his business pure. And of course, once you know some of the things are bad, how can you be sure about any signed material?"

"I was deeply hurt when I found out that he was crooked," said Bob Willig. "If Ken told you that he was only selling to dealers who could afford it, that just isn't true. He sold to people he had befriended and who had befriended him. As things have played out, I can't be sure if he ever felt any remorse at all."

November 19, 1999, was the opening night of the Boston Antiquarian Book Fair, held as always in the Hynes Auditorium on Boylston Street. On the surface, everything seemed fine. Dealers and collectors were walking back and forth, buying and comparing books, or congregating by the bar and casting feigned aspersions at one another.

Also as always, there was plenty of book talk. It became increasingly clear that, just under all this bonhomie, the Ken Anderson affair was far from over. Even with Anderson himself safely under house arrest and the restitution process in the works, the episode had left a deep rift within the antiquarian bookselling community. Dealers were lining up along the moral line of those who had tried to put a stop to Anderson's operation and those who hadn't. A number of those who had been instrumental in publicizing Anderson's activities were bitterly angry at those dealers whom they viewed as having been all too happy to profit by and even abet Anderson's fraud. And, in a most unusual departure from what is ordinarily a remarkably tight-knit and close-mouthed group, those dealers were eager to discuss their grievances and, more than that, were willing to say exactly who it was with whom they were angry.

"There were plenty of people who knew just what they were doing when they bought from Anderson," said John Wronoski, lounging at the bar, making his way through a bottle of Heineken. It was John's e-mail that had alerted Charles Agvent and led eventually to the initials in *The Wasteland*. "There's someone [he named a dealer in western Massachusetts] who's going around now telling everybody that he doesn't remember where he bought his Anderson books, but he remembers just where he got them."

"This is not for attribution," another dealer told us, "but [a preeminent dealer] kept on buying books from Anderson even after being warned. [The owner] said, 'They're too good. I don't believe it.' They weren't *that* good. It's much more a case of not wanting to believe it."

"That is a slanderous lie!" said the accused dealer when we asked for a comment. "I'd love to know who said it so I could sue them! Anyone would be crazy to sell a book that they thought was bad. Nothing could be worse for the business."

"It was more gross stupidity than gross dishonesty," said the first dealer when told of the second dealer's indignation.

As unhealthy for the business as everyone now agrees that selling a bad book is, there are those who think that some of their colleagues did—and are still doing—that very thing.

"There are still plenty of Anderson books around," said Peter Stern. "You can be pretty sure of that."

Another dealer said, "There's one dealer who's being remarkably uncooperative about returning Anderson books. That's because he doesn't want to call his customers and admit that his books were bad and refund the money. Also I think that this dealer may have other Anderson books to sell and doesn't want to turn them in."

John Wronoski was even firmer. "Here, at this fair tonight, is an Anderson book. Not only that, it is the very same Berryman that I was going to buy and that Charles Agvent was going to buy and the dealer who is selling it knows it, but swears it's genuine all the same."

"Lame Duck [John Wronoski's shop] made a mistake by not reporting that dealer to the ABAA," said another member. "The dealer could have been forced to pull the book until it was authenticated." But could they? The ABAA is a voluntary organization. There is no real mechanism for dealing with someone who simply refuses to pull questionable material. Unless the dealer can be shown irrefutably to be selling material he or she knows to be false—a tall order, both morally and legally—any attempt to publicly ostracize a suspected dealer would leave the organization open to a massive lawsuit that, win or lose, would certainly overwhelm the ABAA's limited resources. Although no one has said so specifically, a number of reputable dealers made it plain that they had tried working through the organization with no success.

"We're going to be hearing about this for years," Peter Stern went on. "Maybe not right away. But books are eventually going to be sold by collectors or come up for auction and whoever looks at them is going to say, 'Where did you get this?'"

But the most surprising comment came from Terry Halladay. "It's good that you're doing this," he said. "This situation needs to be aired."

"It's always been a problem with book dealers," said Jim Lowe. "They love to sell signed books, but they never focus on the signature. You know, autographs are something that has always been passed down verbally—what to look for, what to do. At the last New York book fair, there were four signed copies of *Profiles in Courage* for sale—we're talking about books that were priced at between four thousand and seven thousand dollars—and not one of the signatures was Kennedy's. The signatures were secretarial, not even close. And these are reputable dealers. They simply didn't bother to check.

"A collector should never buy an inscribed book without having authentication as a condition of sale," Jim went on. "The argument by dealers of, 'I know what I'm selling because I've been in the business for seventy-five years,' doesn't cut it anymore. The number of people in the business who can properly authenticate a signature is almost nil—maybe ten people in the country. And provenance doesn't help. That just denotes origin. A book can easily be forged, and then make it into a prestigious collection. Provenance means nothing then."

For Jim, there is an obvious answer.

"Book dealers ought to swallow their pride and set up vetting committees. Antique shows do it so that customers who are buying a piece can be reasonably sure it's genuine. But the ABAA won't do it. It's come up before and the idea is always rejected. I don't think a bookshop like [he named a prestigious, high-priced dealer] would put up with someone telling them that a signature is no good."

"That's not the point," Peter Stern responded. "Vetting committees sound like a good idea but they're a complete impossibility. At the New York fair, for instance, do you realize how many pieces are exhibited? It's in the thousands. Most dealers arrive the day before the fair. Who's going to do all that authenticating and when?"

"The real problem," Peter added, "is getting all the dealers to be up-front about what they're selling. If a dust jacket has been professionally restored, for instance, the description should say so. Or that the front endpaper has been replaced. There should either be a card laid in or at least a notation in pencil on the inside. I'm on the board of the Boston fair. No one wants to go up to a dealer and say, 'These books are not really in the condition you're describing.' If anyone tried, the dealer would say, 'What are you picking on me for?' and then name someone else. 'He's worse than me.'"

However one chooses to look at it, if there are dealers out there who are being, at best, less than forthcoming, the ABAA has a problem that threatens the industry it represents.

"For an organization to be worth anything, it has to police its own," Jim Lowe concluded. "It tells the public that we're all reputable people—that we care about what we're selling."

Now that the Ken Anderson affair has come to light, the need, if anything, is even more acute. If you press, any dealer will admit that Anderson was not the only forger out there. At any given time, there are any number of reports of known forgers passing around the book trade—reports that never reach the public—as well as theories about others who haven't been specifically identified yet. All of this, of course, leads to the most important question of all.

Wasn't it possible that a disturbingly large proportion of the books sold to collectors whose value was doubled or tripled because of a signature or inscription were, in fact, fakes?

"No question about it," said Jim Lowe.

In the end, the Anderson affair did more than simply dump some forged inscriptions on the market. It surfaced a fundamental dichotomy in the bookselling business, particularly within the ABAA. It showed first of all that there are dealers like John Crichton, whose high sense of personal and professional honor propels them to extreme lengths on their own time, using their own resources, to keep their industry free of taint. But even John and the others like him seem to hesitate before confronting other dealers whose culpability may be only slightly less than that of Anderson himself.

John said it best in the ABAA newsletter:

> Kenneth Anderson became increasingly expert in his deception and fraud, and we book-sellers were fooled and should be embarrassed. The level of credulity in this case is alarming, and there are serious lessons in this that go to the very heart of our reputation as professionals. Are we in such a hurry to make a profit that we refuse to seriously reflect on the authenticity and credibility of what we are dealing with? . . . Kenneth Anderson was good at what he was doing and getting better, but what came from him was much too good to be true, and it went unquestioned far too long."

Chapter 4

INTO THE TEETH
OF THE FLORIDA BOOK WORLD

*L**ate* one afternoon in mid-fall of 1999, a few months after the publication of *Slightly Chipped: Footnotes in Booklore,* our second book about book collecting, we got a telephone call from a woman in Florida. Her name was Judi Snyder and she said that she was the director of the Blake Library Foundation in Stuart, about forty miles north of Palm Beach. She had seen a review of *Slightly Chipped* in the *Palm Beach Post* and then had gone out and bought the book and loved it.

"We run a book weekend every year, the weekend before the Super Bowl," said Judi. "It's called BookMania! This year it's from January twenty-first to twenty-third. We thought you two would be perfect. We were hoping you could speak on the Sunday."

An invitation to speak to a group is always gratifying for a writer, but never more so than when it comes from a genuinely appreciative reader. For writers whose audience is garnered mainly by word of mouth—like us—these kinds of invitations don't come that often.

While flattered, we had been around long enough not to get overly excited. People outside of the industry might not realize this, but most authors are not reimbursed for travel expenses by their publishers. This means that if you have to travel any distance at all to attend a signing or speaking engagement, the only way to recoup your expenses is by selling books. At a royalty rate of roughly two dollars a book, that can be a tall order, even for a day trip. We've given signings where we've spoken to two people, one of whom was Emily (who can always be counted upon to ask, "How long did it take you to write that book?" during the required question-and-answer period).

Most bookstore owners are aware of this and ask, "Is there a chance you're going to be in the neighborhood?" when soliciting an author for a signing that involves any degree of travel. For our first book, *Used and Rare,* we got one such request for a signing from a bookstore in Cape Cod. It was for the second week in November. "We can get you a deal on a room if you want to stay over and make a kind of holiday of it," the manager said. We were not actually planning on being in Cape Cod during the second week in November. Anyone who has read anything about the Pilgrims knows that Cape Cod can be pretty bleak in the second week of November. On the other hand, maybe there was something we didn't know about contemporary Cape Cod, so we asked what kind of a crowd she could expect.

"Oh, we can always count on getting ten people," she assured us, "sometimes twenty or twenty-five, depending on how bad the weather is." She paused. "I can't guarantee that everyone will buy a book, though."

But before we could tell Judi that we weren't planning on being in Stuart, Florida, in January and, besides, we couldn't possibly find anyone to stay with Emily for an entire weekend, she cut us off. "We'll pay your expenses, of course. We can book your airline tickets from here, and take care of your hotel. We can either get you a rental car or have you picked up at the airport. And, oh yes, just send us receipts for your limousine to and from the airport where you live and we'll reimburse you."

Was there another Goldstone who had a book on the bestseller list that we didn't know about?

"We're very excited about having you," she added.

Florida in January for free? Hey, we were pretty excited too. A plot quickly hatched. "You know, Nancy's parents live in Boca Raton. What if we came down a couple of days early, brought our daughter, left her with them, drove up on the Saturday, then back to Boca on Sunday? Would that be all right?"

"That would be fine," Judi replied, without hesitating for a second.

It got even better. After she booked our airline tickets and rental-car reservation, Judi's travel agent (another member of the Blake Library's extended family) sent us a brochure for the hotel where we would be staying. It was the Marriott Indian River Plantation on Hutchinson Island, which boasted deluxe rooms, two golf courses, thirteen tennis courts, two swimming pools, a private beach, cycling, roller blading, sailing, surfing, and three outdoor bars.

And that wasn't all. When we got the brochure for BookMania 2000!, we found that among our fellow speakers over the three days were award-winning mystery writer Stuart Kaminsky, Oprah Book Club author Jane Hamilton, National Book Award Nominee Amy Bloom, bestselling novelist Elizabeth Berg, and Ming Tsai, star chef and Emmy Award winner for the Food Network's *East Meets West with Ming Tsai*. Others included one of Emily Post's grandchildren, television anchorwoman Mary Alice Williams, and PBS essayist R. Scott Brunner. There were prize-winning children's authors; Ace Atkins, a handsome former football player turned novelist; and Dennis Brown, Angela Lansbury's former publicist, who had spent four years on the road with Gregory Peck. Part of the deal was that all of the guest authors attend a fancy party on Saturday night at a private home just south of Stuart.

We could do that.

Actually, we go to Florida for a family visit almost every year, but almost always during school vacation in March, mostly to bring Emily to see her grandparents. Boca West, the enormous self-contained community where they live, could not be more perfect for the three of them. Emily gets to swim, play at the playground, drive the golf cart (with Papa Ed), go shopping (with Grandma Jackie), putt, drink milkshakes for lunch, and eat spaghetti with butter every night for dinner, all (except for the shopping) without ever having to leave the grounds.

For us, however, while we love getting the family together, and Grandma Jackie and Papa Ed go out of their way to make everything as easy and fun as possible, Boca West . . . well, suffice to say that it wouldn't have been first on our list of vacation hot spots. There are two main reasons for this.

The first is the age of the average Boca West resident. Emily is not the only grandchild who comes there to visit. *Everyone* in Boca West has grandchildren. Great-grandchildren are not uncommon. There is a natural fussiness that is common to this age group, which, at Boca, can sometimes descend to a vague fascism. Boca West has a lot of rules. A guest can't go to the gym until after eleven o'clock in the morning, pretty much can't play tennis without playing doubles, and can't go to the main pool unless accompanied by a member. Nobody gets in without an entry card. You can't eat without a guest card. To get a guest card, you have to go to an office, fill out a form, and get your picture taken. (Fingerprinting and retinal scans aren't due to begin for a couple of years yet.) About the only thing you can do without ID is sit and get a tan at the house you're staying at. Since we, unfortunately, are not lie-in-the-sun-and-soak-up-the-rays sort of people, this has always felt a bit limiting.

Secondly, Boca West is about GOLF. There is virtually no house or condominium in Boca West that does not either abut, face, or back onto a golf course. A good number of patios are screened with wire mesh to keep out bugs and errant tee shots, of which there are many. At eight o'clock every morning, a line of at least fifty golf carts, each with its requisite golf-hatted retirees, is directed on to one of the community's five full-size courses.

We don't play golf.

So, the opportunity to head north for two days, stay at a beautiful ocean-side resort, meet interesting people, and be romantic was decidedly appealing. (The Marriott, as we noted, had two golf courses too, but we were prepared to be broad-minded.)

A few days before we were to leave, completely by coincidence we called John Wronoski at Lame Duck Books to talk about catalogs.

"I can't really talk now," John said. "I've got to pack up for a fair."

"Where are you going this time?" John goes everywhere from Los Angeles to Berlin.

"Fort Lauderdale," he said. "They have a fair at the library. They just got Charles Willeford's papers from his widow. You know Willeford? He's very good. He wrote *Miami Blues,* the one they made into the movie with Alec Baldwin. I'm speaking on Friday night."

"This Friday? We're going to be in Boca," we said. "How's the fair?"

"It's good. It's not that big, but there are a lot of good books. I've been going for ten years. The library collection is interesting too."

This was another surprise. We'd had a singular lack of success in finding places to book-hunt even in the extended vicinity of Boca West. The usually trusty "Book Dealers—Used and Rare" section of the local Yellow Pages had yielded up only a single useful entry, a decent but hardly spectacular used-book store in West Palm Beach.

"We'll see you Friday," we told John.

The Fort Lauderdale Antiquarian Book Fair is held in the lobby of the Broward County Main Library, a modern white marble and

granite building in the center of the city. This is also the home of
the Dianne and Michael Bienes Special Collections and Rare Book
Library, the organization to which the Willeford papers were donated. This was the twelfth year of the fair, which is sponsored by
the Bienes Center, and all profits are used to acquire rare books and
other materials for the collection.

We parked in what seemed to be an honor system parking lot
across the street and went in through the back of the main floor.
The first dealer we encountered was M&M Books of Hollywood,
Florida. Featured above this booth, in eye-popping splendor, was a
large, truly awful painting of a slender young blonde with enormous breasts ("big ones," as they're known in our house), wearing a
revealing blue negligee and blue shawl, both of which were blow-
ing in a stormy wind that did not seem to affect her hair. She was
standing on a cliff overlooking a steep drop and there was a creepy
castle in the background. Under the painting was a little white placard, which read:

Paperback Cover Art
Artist: Robert Maguire
Cover art for Tower Books
(Circa 1960's)
$1600.00

This promised to be an intriguing fair.

The comely vixen in distress was by no means the only beguiling item that M&M Books had to offer. At the top of a small bookcase was a *Psycho* set. It consisted of an original movie lobby card
with Janet Leigh in pink underwear on a bed with a sick green
background, the first printing of the paperback movie tie-in with
Janet screaming against a red background, and the first edition of
the Simon & Schuster 1959 hardcover *Psycho* by Robert Bloch, *An
Inner Sanctum Mystery,* the dust jacket just big white frenzied letters
on a black background, which also came with one of Bloch's signed

"skeleton" book labels laid in underneath. The price for all three was $1250.

We knew that *Psycho* was an expensive book (although the prices of things we can't afford tend to blur) and the book seemed to be in excellent condition, so $1,250 for this set might be a pretty good deal. When we got home to Connecticut, we checked on the Internet to find out just how good a deal it was. We had no trouble finding some comparatives:

BLOCH, Robert, Psycho
NY S&S 1959. First edition. Pages with the inevitable uniform browning and a tiny tear at the crown, else fine in very good plus dustwrapper with a couple of very small chips and tears and a little rubbing. Signed by the author (in ballpoint pen, most signed copies seem to have been signed much later, usually with a marker of some sort). Additionally this copy bears the ownership stamp of the book's dedicatee, and Bloch's literary agent, Harry Altschuler (the printed dedication reads "10% of this book is dedicated to Harry Altschuler, who did 90% of the work"). While it can be assumed that Altschuler owned, and attempted to circulate, more than one copy of this book, this is the closest to a dedication copy of this title we have seen. Basis for the classic Hitchcock film, considered by many critics one of the greatest films in any genre. When Hitchcock determined to film the novel, he instructed his office to attempt to buy up and remove from circulation as many copies as possible, in order not to reveal the nature of the surprise ending, probably contributing greatly to the continued scarcity of the first edition. A very nice copy of a difficult and desirable title.
US$ 2600.00 Between the Covers, ABAA, NJ, U.S.A.

Oh, well, that's a signed copy, you say. Then how about these?

BLOCH, Robert, Psycho
New York: Simon and Schuster, 1959. Publisher's cloth in dust jacket. 185 pp. 8vo. First edition. Near fine; pages a little browned

as usual, in a jacket with only minor edgewear. This poorly constructed book rarely turns up as nice as this.
US$ 1500.00 Jeffrey H. Marks, Rare Books, NY, U.S.A.

BLOCH, ROBERT, Psycho
New York Simon & Schuster 1959 First Edition. Usual slight tanning of pages else fine in a bright dust jacket with a few extremely tiny mends. Attractive copy. The basis of the classic Alfred Hitchcock film.
US$ 1450.00 James Pepper Rare Books, Inc., CA, U.S.A.

Even granting that the poster and paperback together were only worth a few hundred dollars at most, the hardcover (which seemed to be in better condition than any of the three above) was more than worth the price by itself.

To the side of the case holding the *Psycho* set, M&M Books had yet another uncommon display, a table covered with about thirty paperbacks, each encased in a Mylar sleeve. These titles were somewhat less well known:

She didn't know her capacity for love until she read Kinsey
LOVE-STARVED *Woman*
by Peggy Gaddis
An Original Novel

Then there was:

Theirs Was a Passion
No man could share
QUEER AFFAIR

This selection featured a cover depicting two sultry women (both with big ones, of course), one sort of reclining on a couch in a green dress, the second standing up behind her, stroking her cheek.

A man of about forty, in good shape, with a salt-and-pepper beard and hair parted in the middle, wearing a blue tweed sport jacket, jeans, and glasses, saw that notes were being taken, and sidled over.

"What are you writing down? Is this going to be in a newspaper?"

"No, no. My husband and I write about books and I was just, uh, admiring the selection. You're not the owner, by any chance?"

"Yes, I am." He handed over his card. It read:

Michael J. Sellard
First Editions
Vintage Paperbacks
Printed & Pictorial Ephemera

"Hello, Michael. I'm Nancy Goldstone. I wonder if I could ask you some questions?"

"Sure," said Michael.

"How did you get into this business?"

"Oh, the same as other people, I guess. I was collecting and it got out of hand, so I started buying and selling."

"Is there a reason you do mostly paperbacks?"

"Well, vintage paperbacks are in many cases a good alternative for a collector. Take that *Fahrenheit 451*." He indicated a copy on the table. "The paperback is only twenty-nine dollars. An early Bradbury hardcover goes for two or three thousand dollars."

"Well, uh, excuse me for being so ignorant, but I haven't come across these titles before . . ." A wave of the arm encompassed *Queer Affair* and its companions. "You're saying that this collection reflects your taste? You've read all these books, then?"

"NONONONONO," he said, waving his arms. "You collect vintage paperbacks for the *cover art*. *That's* what it's all about. Beacon, Midwood—those are the publishers." He leaned forward. "The lesbian paperbacks are so popular I can't afford them anymore," he said.

Just across from M&M was Barrister Books, owned, it said on the placard at the booth, by Sheldon and Rosalind Kurland from Davie, about twenty minutes southwest of Boca Raton. Barrister had one of the larger displays, with one entire case of modern firsts, and two more of nonfiction, with an emphasis on history. Whenever we come across a new dealer, we try to find some books with whose prices we're familiar to get a sense of things. Right in the middle of Barrister's modern-first bookcase was a pristine signed copy of *Snow Falling on Cedars*. It's a book that's fairly common—David Guterson, the author, signed a lot of books—and it usually sells in the $175 to $200 range. We've seen it for as much as $250. Barrister Books was selling it for $140, a good sign.

Then, on the top shelf, we saw a copy of Saul Bellow's fourth book, *Seize the Day*. This book is not particularly rare but we'd been looking for a copy for a couple of years. The spine is almost always sunned, as in this copy, but even so, a first edition generally goes for close to $100, with a dealer like Between the Covers weighing in at $150. Barrister Books was selling its copy, in very good shape except for the mild fading, for $30.

"Sheldon is an attorney," said Ros Kurland, a woman in her fifties with short black hair, who was manning the booth. "He specializes in taxes, wills, estates, elder law . . ." (no small potatoes in Florida). "I teach special ed to grades one through five."

The Kurlands work exclusively out of their home and don't even have a Web site. They started, as had Michael Sellard and almost every other dealer at this fair, as collectors whose acquisitive bent had gotten out of hand.

"I told him he couldn't buy anymore unless he sold some books," said Ros flatly.

We assumed that the Kurlands had named their business after Sheldon's profession.

"No," said Ros. "Actually we named it after our dog. We met when we were both at the University of Miami. The day my husband was sworn in as a member of the bar, we bought a German shepherd and named him Barrister." Ros's face tightened into a frown. "A kennel killed him. We used to leave him at the same place every time we went away. One time, while we were on vacation, the kennel was sold. At that time, Florida had no law regulating kennels. When we came back, we found out that Barrister had been killed. We sued and put the guy out of business. We gave the money to our kids."

The seemingly omnipresent John Wronoski was at the next booth over. "I've been coming to this fair since it started," he said. "I used to come with Tom Congalton [of Between the Covers] but after a while he decided it wasn't worth his while to make the trip. But it's a good fair and my family likes it down here, so I come every year."

The fair wasn't large, only about fifteen booksellers in all. As we looked around, we realized that, apart from John, there wasn't a single dealer there whom we'd ever heard of before. It soon became clear why we'd been having so much trouble finding shops in the area in which to browse—only two or three of the dealers were in the business full-time. Like the Kurlands, just about everyone else had day jobs and ran their book operations out of their home. Although most had Web sites, few advertised in the Yellow Pages. Some had no means of identification at all.

"I'm sorry we don't have a card," said Glennis LeBlanc, who with her husband Thomas Fink was standing in front of a booth identified as The Missing Volume. "We just got into the business. This is only our second show."

They were both in their twenties. Glennis had her hair back and was wearing a cable-knit sweater. Thomas had a beard like Trotsky and was wearing boots and a double-breasted black leather jacket, which was unzipped and hanging open. They looked like a couple of beat poets who were just stopping by on their way to Greenwich Village.

"I work for Charles Schwab," said Thomas, "and Glennis is in human resources for a computer company. We met at a bookstore."

"We were both working at Walden Books," she said. "We get a lot of our books from England."

"I go there a lot on business," said Thomas.

"Yeah," added Glennis. "The airlines love us. We come back with five bags of books. We're overweight with just one of them. When we got married, we started The Missing Volume."

Their selection of UK firsts was quite good, including a number of advance reading copies of authors like Iain Banks. There were also a number of first UKs of American titles, such as *Cold Mountain,* and a number of UK editions of Carl Hiaasen (who is obviously very popular in Florida). Personally, we often prefer UK editions of American books because the dust jackets are more fun, a little bit more off-center than their American counterparts.

Here again, reflecting The Missing Volume's limited overhead, the prices were terrific.

Right next door was Kathmandu Books. Kathmandu had a larger selection, heavily weighted toward science fiction, mystery, and fantasy, but also with some unusual examples of other kinds of fiction. Some of the titles were *Audrey Hepburn's Neck* by Alan Brown and *Buddy Holly: Alive and Well on Ganymede* by Bradley Denton. We saw a first of *Searching for Bobby Fischer* and scarce first UKs of books by Carlos Perez-Reverte.

The proprietor was also young—early thirties it seemed. He was wearing a printed shirt, *very* white sneakers, and a Mickey Mouse watch. He said his name was Mark Wingenfeld and that he had been in the business for three years. As with Glennis and Thomas and the Kurlands, bookselling was a sideline.

"I'm with Siemens," he said. "It's Siemens-Westinghouse now. I've been there nine years. I design gas and steam turbines. I've been reading science fiction since I was ten years old," he said. "But I read all kinds of fiction now."

Mark shows at local fairs but is about to become more ambitious. "I'm going to Chicago in September," he said, "for the world science fiction conference." He paused and looked up. "Is this for print? Am I going to be reading about myself in a newspaper?"

We told him no, that we were taking notes for a book. Then we introduced ourselves.

"Oh!" he said, with a flash of recognition. "Now I get it. I have your book at home." He dropped his eyes. "I have to confess that I haven't been able to find time to read it yet. I only got through the first chapter so far . . . but I really liked it." He smiled. "I guess I'll have to read the rest now."

We spent a little more time browsing. ("Be careful how you use that word," John Wronoski told us. "*Browse* comes from Old English and means 'to break.' ") For us, who are used to seeing the same dealers at every regional fair in our area, this fair reminded us of the diversity of tastes in the book world. It was very refreshing. Also, this might have been the last place in America where you could buy an as-new first of *Cold Mountain* for $125.

After we'd talked to John on the telephone, we pulled up some material on the Bienes Collection, then called the librarian, Jim Findlay, and asked if we could meet with him while we were at the fair. Jim was sitting at a table near the stairs, with various brochures of library services and programs in front of him. We guessed he was in his early fifties, but he had a deep tan, a buzz-haircut, chiseled features, and a trim build, and looked more like a senior Olympian than a librarian. He was wearing a black-and-white checked sport jacket, a black-and-white checked tie, and black pants. He had a full mustache and glasses.

"We had a lot more dealers last year," he said, nodding toward the fair. "It's the Internet. The library feels it also. We have fewer and fewer patrons. People find their information on the computer, especially easy reference material. If you want to find out something about Emily Dickinson, say, you can find a Web site and get everything you want without leaving the house.

"Of course, you won't get the kind of depth you'll find at the library but . . ." he shrugged.

We took an elevator to the fourth floor. "The Bienes Library is the headquarters of the Florida Center for the Book," Jim continued. "About ten or twelve years ago, the Library of Congress started establishing state centers to promote books and reading, and Florida was the first state to take advantage of the program. The Florida State Center for the Book promotes Florida authors and books through programs, exhibitions, author workshops, and mystery writer workshops."

When the doors opened, Jim made a left and led us to a pair of locked double glass doors. There were tables and chairs inside, each table cluttered with piles of papers. There were also little stacks of books, boxes, and ephemera on the floor. "This is the rare-book room," he said, opening the doors. "Also my office. Please excuse the mess. I'm putting together a couple of exhibits."

"I always like to have something going on," said Jim as we walked inside. He led us to the packages on the floor. "Here's something that might interest you. These are submissions for this year's Florida Arts Book Prize. I started this a couple of years ago. We give out a two-thousand-dollar prize each year for the winning entry. It is just open to Florida residents. Mostly, professional artists enter original books. The purpose is to encourage artists to use books as an art form." He opened one of the boxes. Inside was a small metal box with an unlocked clasp. The box had been paper lined, so that when it was opened, the contents were raised up. "See? This is from a woman who put together all of her family's passports into a book." He showed us another entry, whose cover seemed to be a bird feather encased in Mylar. When he opened the Mylar, the feathers spread out so that the cover became a soaring bird. A third entry had an art deco–esque cityscape that opened in sections. They weren't all great, but each was a very personal statement by the artist who created it.

"I'll be judging these along with some professional collectors," said Jim. "We have people from both the book side and the art side. This has really caught on. Each year we get a lot more entries.

"My own background is in art, so I try to diversify," said Jim. "I don't want to do just moldy old books. I put on a Duane Hanson exhibit, and an exhibit of the Miami ballet, featuring costumes, drawings, sets . . . we also ran an eighteenth-, nineteenth-, and twentieth-century exhibit of slave and antislave literature and art. Look at this." He took us to a glass display case, which featured an old, lined book open to a random page. "This is a ledger book from 1870. It contains the names of the members of the African Society. They were freed black women. It records their names and the dues they paid."

There was a poster on another table. It was called "The Anti-Slavery Constitutional Amendment Picture," and was printed in 1865. It pictured Abraham Lincoln, and Vice President Hannibal Hamlin, and had small photographs of every congressman who had voted for the Fourteenth Amendment.

Jim led us over to a glass case where some primitive-looking, scary hand puppets were placed next to little kits that gave instructions on how to make them. It turned out that the puppets were not from a tribe deep in the Amazon, but rather from the United States in the 1930s. The crimson one with the demonic face was "The Red Nerve," and the evil olive one was "The Green Germ." There was a blue germ, too. They were all intended to be part of "The Big Show," a production that also included a friendly-looking, middle-aged dentist puppet, a skirt-and-heels-clad mother puppet, a kindly grandfather puppet, and a very clean-cut *Leave It to Beaver*-looking boy puppet.

"This was all done during the depression," said Jim, "as part of the WPA. WPA literature and related material are our most important collection. We have over sixteen hundred titles in our collection—it's the best in the United States."

The WPA, of course, was one of the most interesting social experiments in American history. It was started in 1935, as one of the showpieces of the New Deal, and was intended to provide work for those with skills important to society who could not otherwise make a living. For perhaps the first time in our nation's history, included in this definition of essential Americans were artists, writers—even actors. The WPA funded such enterprises as the Federal Theater Project, the Federal Arts Project, and the Federal Writers' Project.

Since this was the Depression, there was none of that old pick-your-project-and-apply-for-a-grant routine favored by today's NEA supporters. The WPA was for the common good, at least the common good as defined by FDR's minions. Those who qualified were paid to go from place to place, often living in little socialist camps, and do whatever the project's administrators deemed appropriate in their particular field that would benefit the larger society. If you were a writer, you wrote—but it could be a handbook on how to butcher a cow. If you were a painter, you painted, even if it was signposts or the walls of railroad stations. And, since there were some pretty talented starving artists around in those days, you got some pretty bohemian railroad stations, like the one in New Jersey that, after coats of paint were removed years later, was revealed to have a mural painted by the Armenian-born surrealist Arshile Gorky that was worth over a million dollars.

The reason that an Arshile Gorky masterpiece could escape detection was that almost everything was done anonymously—another one of those little egalitarian touches that made Franklin Roosevelt so popular with conservatives. That's what makes it so difficult to figure out today if those helpful hints in the *How to Use a Vacuum Cleaner* pamphlet were written by Zora Neale Hurston, Studs Terkel, or Vardis Fisher, all of whom worked for the WPA.

Jim then took us into the stacks. We saw shelves filled with hundreds of books, each only about four inches high. It looked like the main library in Munchkinland.

"This is our Big Little Book collection," Jim explained. "Do you know what a Big Little Book is? They were sold in five-and-dime stores in the 1930s, '40s, and '50s. They're children's picture books."

It was an eclectic selection. There was the usual assortment of cartoon characters popular with kids of the forties and fifties, like *Little Orphan Annie* and *Dick Tracy*. But a number of other titles reflected a different mood of the period. *G-Man vs. The Red,* for example.

All in all, the collection was extraordinary for a small public library. More than that, you could feel the commitment of Jim and his staff. The level of innovation was startling. (Upon our return home, we immediately called the president of the Friends of the Westport Library and encouraged her to rip off as many of these ideas as possible.)

"Five years ago," said Jim, "Fort Lauderdale was a cultural wasteland. Now, there's a new opera house, an art museum, a museum of science . . . this is a very supportive community.

"We have a Web site where we post what we're doing," he added, "so that other libraries can use us as a resource. So, you see, the benefits become larger than the library."

After we were done, we returned to the ground floor for one last quick look at the book fair. On the way out, we noticed a thriving gift shop, a restaurant that was almost full, people everywhere, not just at the fair, and a general feeling of energy in the place. Here it was, a beautiful, warm, sunny Friday in January, and all of these people had chosen to come to the library instead of the beach. Between this and what they were doing at the Blake Library, there was clearly something going on in southern Florida that we had missed all these years.

Buoyed by the morning, we headed over to Las Olas Boulevard and found ourselves a little bistro, where we sat outside, had great *panini*s and some very decent house wine, watched people stroll by, and slipped into the romantic mood that we were looking forward to carrying with us for the entire weekend.

We woke up the next morning and decided that Fort Lauderdale had been a good omen. Up until then, all the first-class treatment notwithstanding, we had been a little anxious about our speaking date in Stuart. When Judi had first told us that we were scheduled to speak at two o'clock on Sunday, the time had held no particular significance but, then, the previous weekend, we had realized that there were going to be a couple of other events conflicting with our little talk.

Judi had said that the Blake held BookMania! the weekend before the Super Bowl to coincide with the traditional bye week in the NFL. "Otherwise, everyone might stay home and watch football." But this year, unbeknownst to the Blake people when they had scheduled the event, there *was* no bye week. That Sunday was the day of the NFL Conference Championships, two games back-to-back to determine the participants in the Super Bowl.

And, just to make things perfect, for the first time ever, each of these games had a Florida team playing—Jacksonville early, Tampa Bay late.

(We seem to have an unerring knack for this sort of bad timing. The year before, one of us had a signing for his novel on the very same evening *and at the very same time* as the final episode of *Seinfeld.* When one of our friends heard about this, she called and said, "You're not going head-to-head with *SEINFELD,* are you?" But there was nothing to be done and the signing went ahead as scheduled. Of course, that had been in Westport, our hometown, where we were able to at least beg, cajole, or flatter enough of our friends to make a showing. Still, as one after another of the draftees marched in, just after the warm smiles in the direction of the lectern, we could hear frantic whispering back and forth: "You're taping it, aren't you? You're taping it, aren't you?")

But now, football be damned. We were *enthused.* After all, not *everyone* watches the NFL. Even in football-crazy Florida, there must be *some* people who would rather talk about books than watch two local teams battle to participate in one of the preeminent sporting events in the world, right?

Although we weren't required to be in Stuart for the Saturday cocktail party until seven o'clock in the evening, we kissed everyone at Boca good-bye and left at eleven in the morning in order to pack every last romantic second into the trip. Our plan was to get to the resort, have an intimate, sophisticated lunch, walk along the beach, then maybe have a Planter's Punch at one of those little outdoor bars, catch one of the other authors' presentations, spend a little married time in the room later, laze around with a bath or Jacuzzi, and then make our way to the cocktail party.

We had been told that the trip from Boca Raton would take about an hour and a half, but the Florida Turnpike has a seventy-mile-an-hour speed limit and there was no traffic. It was a beautiful, sunny, not-too-hot afternoon and, as we drove through the local streets heading toward the ocean, we relaxed into the moment. We were literally five minutes away from the hotel, on the second of two causeways that link Hutchinson Island to the mainland, waiting while the drawbridge rose to allow a couple of enormous sailboats to pass underneath, when all of a sudden—

"Oh my God! I can't believe it!"

"What is it, Larry?"

"Oh my God, I can't believe this!"

"What? What? Are you all right?"

"My tooth just broke off!!!"

"What?"

"My tooth just broke in half! Right in front!"

"You're kidding."

"Oh, yeah? Look!"

Silence. Then: "Does it hurt?"

"No, it doesn't hurt. But look at me! Right in front!"

Pause. "Well, it's not *right* in front. It's one over from the front."

"Oh, I suppose I should be relieved it's not *right* in front."

Soothingly. "It doesn't look so bad."

"DOESN'T LOOK SO BAD! ARE YOU NUTS!? IT
LOOKS LIKE I'M FROM THE OZARKS OR SOMETHING!"

"You don't have to yell at me."

"I'M NOT YELLING AT YOU!"

"Larry, really, it's really not that noticeable. Just try not to open
your mouth too wide."

"Oh, great. I'm supposed to speak with my mouth closed."

"Believe me. No one will notice."

"You're out of your mi . . . hey, wait a minute. It fits."

"What do you mean, 'It fits?'"

"It broke clean. I can put it back in. It doesn't really stay but
maybe I can get a dentist to cement it in. It only has to hold for a
couple of days. A dentist could do it, right?"

"Well, it's Saturday. . . ."

"Thanks for the encouragement."

"But I'm sure the people at the hotel can a find a dentist."

"You think so?"

"Sure."

"Jeeez, I can't believe this happened to me. Our romantic
weekend."

(Actually, this is the G-rated version. The one with the broken
tooth, understandably upset, was using somewhat saltier language.
There was a good deal of moaning too.)

"Don't worry. It will all be fine. Let's just get to the hotel."

The drawbridge finally went down and we made it across. The
hotel was just over the causeway and we screeched into the parking
lot.

"Are you sure you're okay?"

"WILL YOU PLEASE STOP ASKING ME THAT?! I'M
FINE."

"Okay, okay. How's your tooth?"

"I'm holding it in place with my tongue."

We went inside. There were two young women behind the desk.

"May I help you?" one asked pleasantly.

"Goldstone. We're checking in. Look—"

"Goldstone . . . Goldstone . . . Lawrence and Nancy?"

"Yes. Look—"

"You're with the Blake Library?"

"Yes, look I—"

"You were supposed to be here yesterday."

"No we weren't."

"Yes you were. We have a reservation for you for yesterday and today."

"I don't care! Listen, I need to see a dentist. It's an emergency."

"A dentist? It's Saturday."

"I know, I know, but I have to speak tomorrow. We're going to have our pictures taken. Not everyone is going to watch the game, you know."

"Huh?"

"Never mind. Can you please try to find me a dentist?"

"What kind of emergency is it?"

"My tooth broke! Look!" The tooth was removed and held out for the woman's inspection.

The woman flinched, grimaced, tried gamely to smile, and then grabbed for the phone.

"Are you in pain?" asked the other woman.

A man had come in behind us to register. He was in his forties, had long hair that fell over his forehead, and was carrying a white PVC fiddle case and a white PVC tube closed up at both ends with the screw-ins that plumbers use to close off drainpipes. He was also apparently one of the speakers for BookMania!

The man had overheard our conversation and turned to us. "If you're in pain, maybe I can help. I know a lot about mouth pain." He spoke in a soft, modulated drawl and looked and sounded like a young Shelby Foote. "I've got some things for pain management," he added.

"No, that's all right," we replied foolishly, not even bothering to inquire just what it was that he had for pain management. "It doesn't hurt. It just looks awful." The tooth was once more removed for examination.

The man flinched, grimaced, tried gamely to smile, then took his room key and left.

The women behind the desk were wonderful. They called 1-800-DENTIST. After asking for everything but the color of the patient's underwear, the 1-800-DENTIST operator said that none of their dentists in the area would see a patient on Saturday, even in an emergency. Next, the women behind the desk scoured the Yellow Pages. For the next half hour, they called every single dentist within a forty-five-minute drive of the hotel. No one. Not one single dentist in all of Stuart, Florida, would take an emergency on a Saturday.

"You're lucky it doesn't hurt," said one of the women.

We went up to our room and, desperate, called our own dentist back in Westport, hoping to be able to eventually track down whoever was on call. Adam Freeman—great guy, wonderful dentist, good-looking—took the call himself. *He* was working on Saturday. "I always work on Saturdays," he said. "Not all of my patients can make it during the week." Now *that's* a dentist. Adam listened to the problem.

"Get yourself some Krazy Glue," he advised. "Dry both surfaces as best you can. Use one drop, just one drop."

"Krazy Glue?"

"We sometimes use it as a tissue adhesive, except we don't call it Krazy Glue. That should hold you until you get back. Try not to chew on it. And Larry . . ."

"Yes?"

"Make sure you don't get any on your lip."

They didn't have any Krazy Glue for sale, but the woman in the gift shop had a tube, which she let us borrow. We dried off both surfaces with a paper towel, put one drop on the broken half, and stuck it in.

It worked.

We were still a little shaken but, once again, tentatively optimistic. We gave the woman back her glue, had a small, careful, tooth-obsessed, soft-food lunch, and then took a walk on the beach.

Sure enough, just off the beach entrance was a little outdoor bar. We found ourselves a table and ordered a couple of Planter's Punches and settled in. Just then, the man from the desk with the PVC cases wandered into the bar area and sat at another table. We invited him to join us.

His name was Scott Ainslee and he was a blues historian, musician, and singer from Durham, North Carolina. He had written a history of the legendary blues artist Robert Johnson, who had been shot down by a lover's husband in 1937, but whose music had been used by a number of contemporary groups, including the Rolling Stones.

Pretty soon we got to the important question. "Just what is it that you have for pain management?" we asked.

"Oh," he said, "nothing like that. But mouth pain can be controlled pretty well with acupuncture. You can even do it with a fingernail. Acupuncture is better for some things than for others—doesn't do diddley for abdominal stuff. But mouth pain . . . definitely."

"Oh."

Scott ordered a drink and we swapped stories for a while. When we told him the title of our book, he grinned slyly, gestured tooth-ward, and said, "I guess you really are Slightly Chipped."

The cocktail party was called for seven-thirty. By seven, thanks to Scott and the Planter's Punches, we had regained some sense of normalcy. We hadn't made it all the way back to romantic, but at least we had moved some distance above horrible.

We drove to yet another gated community—southern Florida seems to be a series of fortresses separated by Publix supermarkets and Denny's—and immediately found ourselves in a line of cars, all going to the same place, a large, low-slung house. There were three hustling young valet parkers in front. At the door were the hostesses, a short gracious woman in her sixties with bright red hair, and a trim gray-haired woman from the board of the Blake Foundation. We introduced ourselves and were ushered inside.

The living room was large and elegant and there were already knots of people standing around. Outside, by the pool, there was a bar manned by two bartenders, and to the right was another room that seemed to contain food.

We checked out the crowd. Stuart Kaminsky was on a couch, in an animated discussion with a woman in her eighties. Jane Hamilton was sweeping through the room in a long skirt. Ace Atkins seemed free but one of us was certain that he'd be boring.

We realized immediately that there was an unspoken etiquette at this party. It was clear that the celebrity authors were reserved for those who had contributed large amounts of money to be there. Second-level authors, like us, were left to strike up conversations with unoccupied guests or each other.

Since we'd eaten minimally at lunch, we decided to get some food first. It was, to say the least, a lavish spread. At a large round table were dozens of appetizers—sushi, dumplings, barbecued chicken wings, bite-sized pizza canapés, puff pastry stuffed with crabmeat, at least six different kinds of cheese and crackers, and two large standing pineapples covered all over with cocktail shrimps stuck on with toothpicks. To the side was a man standing behind a small table serving miniature roast beef sandwiches and tiny lamb chops with mint sauce. There was a separate round table for desserts, with individual pecan pies, chocolate truffles, fruit tarts, cookies, brownies, and strawberries dipped in chocolate.

(We don't want to belabor this, but at the first bite, the tooth broke again. KRAZY GLUE TIP: When they say to dry both surfaces *thoroughly,* they mean it. We borrowed some more glue from the host, repaired to the bathroom, almost dropped the tooth fragment down the drain, went through some extensive gyrations to tenuously reattach it, and then returned to the party. Are we a couple of troupers, or what?)

Unsure whether or not the tooth was going to fall off in someone's drink, we decided to ease our way into the festivities. A woman in her early thirties was bending over, examining the crabmeat puffs. She seemed like the sympathetic type, so we started with her. Like just about everyone there, she was a contributor to the Blake Library Foundation.

"There's no state income tax in Florida—saying 'taxes' here is like saying 'abortion' in the Vatican. Anyway, because of that, public libraries like the Blake are almost completely dependent upon private contributions. That's the reason for the foundation.

"It's good in some ways, I suppose, and bad in others. It gets the community involved in the library—that means that, in addition to contributing money, people from the area probably use the library more than if it was just here and they could take it for granted."

A woman holding a camera came up to us. She had come with Dennis Brown, the former publicist who had written *Actor's Talk: Profiles and Stories from the Acting Trade.* She insisted we meet him and brought us over to where Dennis was standing with another man, who turned out to be R. Scott Brunner, the National Public Radio commentator who had written a memoir entitled *Due South: Dispatches from Down Home.* Scott had already given his talk at the library that afternoon.

"How did it go?" we asked.

"Very well," Scott replied. "They sold out of all my books."

That sounded promising. "When do you go?" we asked Dennis.

"At eleven o'clock tomorrow. At least I'll be done before the

game starts," he said, exhaling deeply to demonstrate profound relief. "What about you?"

"Two," we replied tersely.

Put a couple of Yankees (us) together with a man from a border state (Dennis) and another from the South (Scott), and guess
what is the first topic of conversation?

"Ken Burns had everything wrong," said Dennis. "Real Civil
War scholars hate that series. The war started for a lot of reasons
other than slavery, but you'd never know it by watching PBS."

Scott (whose day job, it turned out, was in real estate) took a
more measured view but did agree that Southerners were less ec-
static in their praise of *The Civil War* than were Northerners. We
asked how he began doing radio commentary.

"It started locally," he said. "I submitted some pieces to our local NPR station. They were each about two minutes, meant to be
read aloud. Even if they used them, I didn't think they'd ask me to
read them, but they did. Other stations eventually picked them up,
mostly in the South. Every once in a while, I get one that goes national."

The next morning, we decided to go and hear Dennis speak. He
had been intelligent and funny the night before and seemed to have
any number of anecdotes about the theater people he'd interviewed.
He'd spent months on the road with Gregory Peck.

It was a big auditorium, with a stage and a microphone and
seating for at least two hundred, but there were only thirty or so
people in the audience. Dennis, as he had been at the cocktail party,
was a polished and engaging speaker, and his stories of actors and
their profession were witty and revealing. At the end of his talk, he
pointed in our direction, asked us to stand, and then said what
wonderful speakers we were, how interesting our book was, and
that everyone there should make sure to come back and hear us. Although grateful for the plug, we watched the thirty or so people

nod and smile, which we took for, "You think I'm going to miss football for *them?*"

We left the auditorium, got in the car, and drove around, going over what we were going to say. We started with the obligatory opening anecdote. For this talk, we had chosen—appropriately, it seemed—"The Worst Book Signing Story Ever." It's something we had heard from Maggie Topkiss at Partners & Crime, a mystery-bookstore in New York. We've never been sure if it is really true, but it is such a great story that we tell it anyway.

It's about George Dawes Green, whose second book, *The Juror,* was made into a hugely successful film. When Green's first book, *The Caveman's Valentine,* came out, it received excellent reviews and an Edgar for Best First Mystery, but next to no publicity. Green was eager for any opportunity he could find to publicize his book, so when his publisher told him that they had arranged a signing in some suburb of Boston—Woburn or some such place—Green agreed to drive up from New York, even though it was the middle of January. Five minutes out of the city, the heater in his car broke down and he spent the rest of the four-hour drive freezing. (Remember, they don't pay for hotels, so, afterward, he had to drive back, too.)

When he got to the bookstore, they had set up a podium with a stack of his books and a poster and about thirty chairs. Only one of these was occupied—by a woman still bundled up in her parka. What the hell, Green thought, I'm here already, so, for an hour, he gave the woman a private reading, and then answered all of her questions. Finally, when her curiosity was exhausted, she stood up to leave.

"Thank you very much," she said. "I only came in because I live across the street and my boiler isn't working. But your book sounds very interesting and if it ever comes out in paperback, maybe I'll buy a copy."

As we headed back to the Blake Library, we hoped that, in the future, when we told the worst book-signing story ever, it wouldn't be ours.

We walked back in about one-thirty. Someone else was speaking and the doors to the auditorium were closed, so we couldn't tell what the attendance was like. There were some people in the library, but they seemed to be there on regular business—homework, reading to children, checking out the Sunday papers, that sort of thing. As we had feared, there didn't seem to be anyone there at all for us. Even our family hadn't yet arrived.

The library staff had set up a greenroom for its speakers and we were whisked into it, to ensure, we were convinced, that we didn't try to run out on them. There were soft drinks and cheese and crackers and a big bowl of Honey Belle oranges. The last meal.

They had a couple of people in the room to chat with us until, finally, one of the volunteers poked her head through the door. "Ready to speak?" she asked with assaulting good cheer. "Come with me. Judi's just about to introduce you."

We followed the woman to the auditorium. Judi was up on the stage, a microphone in her hand. "Our next speakers write charming memoirs about their obsession with books and book collecting," she said. "Please welcome Lawrence and Nancy Goldstone."

Suddenly there was applause and we found ourselves walking down the aisle to the podium. And, hey, there were people, at least fifty or sixty, which is quite a lot by our standards. And right up in the front row in the center sat our daughter and her grandparents, all beaming.

It went wonderfully. Everyone laughed at the worst book-signing story ever, although we are aware that now that we have blabbed in print, we can't use it anymore. We read from our books, told our stories, and had a terrific time. We even told the tooth story (although the fragment was not removed for the benefit of the audience). Afterwards we sat at a table in the hall and signed books and talked to people who, like us, relish reading and the hunt for old books.

Writing can be a brutal business. A writer can work for years on something only to find that no one will publish it, or if someone does publish it, that it gets horrific reviews or sells ten copies. And when your book is rejected, so is a piece of your soul. We know this sounds melodramatic, but every writer we've ever heard about, including some who are wildly successful, feel precisely this way.

So when we can go to something like BookMania! and be greeted by an appreciative audience filled with people who enjoyed reading what we had worked so hard to produce—well, there is simply nothing better.

$\mathcal{C}$hapter 5

BOOKS@PROFIT.COM

$\mathcal{S}$oon after we began writing about books, we also began to receive book catalogs regularly in the mail. These came not
only from dealers from whom we had purchased something, but
also from a lot of dealers we had never heard of. We like to think
that is because those dealers had read and enjoyed our work, but it
is more likely that they had targeted us as potentially eager customers.

Book catalogs are not like the catalogs you get from Home Depot or Victoria's Secret, full of beguiling pictures of radial-arm saws
or leopard-skin lounge wear. But what you do sometimes get are
choice little annotations that are included to give background to a
particular book's subject (and to justify what is often a lofty price).
These can be great fun, even if you don't buy anything. Here are
just a few of the tidbits we've garnered from catalogs:

- Benjamin Franklin, patriot, discoverer of electricity, and general all-around American hero, preferred older women to
  younger ones, on the grounds that "every Knack being by
  Practice, capable of Improvement."

- General John "Gentleman Johnny" Burgoyne was forced to face the entire British parliament and issue an explanation of why he lost to the American colonists at Saratoga, the text of which was then printed in a pamphlet. His explanation apparently unsatisfactory, he was tossed out of the army and took his revenge by becoming a successful playwright.
- The screenplay for *Lawrence of Arabia* was originally written by Terence Rattigan. The film, which was to be directed by Anthony Asquith and star Dirk Bogarde, was within days of shooting before being scuttled.
- Sinclair Lewis once went on a thirty-six-hour drinking binge with his English publisher, A. S. Frere, which ended with the two of them barging into the United States Naval Academy, where Lewis introduced Frere as a general of the Royal Flying Corps and commandeered a full cadet review.

We've also seen listings for a lock of Abraham Lincoln's hair, Jack Kerouac's college term paper, and seeds collected by Charles Darwin.

And then there's this, perhaps our all-time favorite:

ONDAATJE, MICHAEL.
Michael Ondaatje's 1974 Wall Calendar. Toronto: 1974. Ondaatje's own wall calendar for the year 1974 which is extensively annotated by him in his hand as to his family's activities on an often daily basis. The calendar is entitled "Milk Calendar" showing color pictures of the many uses of milk. Used and thumbed, an interesting look at an author's life as well as his relationship to his family. . . .
$250.

We continue to be fascinated by this item. How does one decide how much to charge for an old wall calendar, even Michael Ondaatje's wall calendar? How useful is it to know that on Thursday, April 14, he picked up his dry cleaning at 3:00 and took the girls to ballet at 4:30? What insight into *The English Patient* can be gained by knowing the exact time and date that Mr. Ondaatje was expecting the exterminator? And, of course, the most pressing question—what is the significance of milk in Mr. Ondaatje's work?

Apart from the occasional tidbit that will surface in almost any catalog, there are some dealers who consistently inform, entertain, or both, although booksellers have widely different approaches in presenting material in such a way as to make it irresistible.

Between the Covers, a high-end dealer in modern firsts—about as high as it gets—is always entertaining. The cover of each catalog features a clever, Saul Steinberg–esque color painting by a man named Tom Bloom, and is almost always accompanied by Bloom song lyrics, witty asides, or, occasionally, Bloom verse. Catalog 61 featured this ode:

> Welcome to this little burg
> Devoted to the printed word
> Its citizenry is made up of books
> And it's calm and collected as it looks
> The rave reviews you read in blurbs
> Reach all the way out to the burbs
> But for the details exposed on the flaps
> This town does not exist on any maps
> So plan a trip, come and stay
> A year, a month, a week, a day
> It's the same yet different from the others
> It's name?
> BETWEEN THE COVERS

They don't scrimp on production costs either. Their catalogs are printed on rich, glossy stock and inside, in addition to the listings, many of the dust jackets are reproduced in rich, glossy, full-color photographs. Although there seems to be a ten-dollar charge just to receive each catalog, they've never billed us. "We try to be whimsical with our catalogs," said Tom Congalton, one of the owners of Between the Covers. "Of course, some people say that our prices are whimsical too."

Once, Between the Covers did a joint mailing with Biblioctopus of California that definitely won the whimsy prize. Instead of the standard book form, the catalog came in a hard plastic case, 2¾ x 3½ inches, with a snap-open top. Inside was a wraparound sleeve, made to look like a leather-bound book, with "Classic Book Cards" printed on the spine. The sleeve was filled with seventy-six little cards, each of which was a listing for a book or set. On the front of each card was a full-color image of the dust jacket, and there was a description and price on the back.

A printed note was enclosed. It read:

> We would like you to have this complimentary set of Classic Book Cards, a catalog of rare books which has been jointly produced by Biblioctopus of Century City, CA and Between the Covers of Merchantville, NJ. We realize that you'll probably want to run right out and begin trading them with your friends, or threading them between the spokes of your bicycle wheels, but please note: THESE BOOKS ARE AVAILABLE FOR AND ARE BEING OFFERED FOR SALE. And you can always say you bought the Classic Book Cards copy! What could be better?
>
> P.S. Additional sets are available for holiday gift giving at $20 per set, postpaid.

Classic Book Card Number 1 was a first edition of *The Old Man and the Sea,* in condition described as "fine/fine," with a price of $1,750 (which was the most we'd ever seen this go for unsigned) and the last card, Number 76, was a near-fine/very good first of *The Maltese Falcon,* priced at $25,000, also a reasonably aggressive price, even for so rare a book.

Of the seventy-six cards, only a handful were for books priced under $1,000. Many were over $10,000, with the high being $150,000 for Classic Book Card Number 38, the three-volume first

UK edition of *The Whale,* which, when released in the United States was, of course, retitled *Moby-Dick.* On the back it read:

> 1st edition, preceding the American, 3 vols, the leviathan of triple deckers, 1st binding of blue cloth sides and creamy white spines with gilt whales. A fine set, beautiful beyond good fortune. If you start your Melville collection with this book, put a fork in yourself cause you're done. Full morocco case.

Now if that doesn't get you to go out and plunk down your 150 big ones, nothing will.

On the other end of the spectrum from whimsy, there is John Wronoski at Lame Duck Books—"the Duck," as he is known to cognoscenti. ("When I was starting out, I was interested in birds so I was looking for a self-disparaging ornithological name," John noted.) Before he became a rare-book dealer, John had run a small scholarly used-book shop and, if he wasn't producing book catalogs, he might be writing college textbooks. In fact, some of the Lame Duck catalogs are so detailed that you could probably get college credit just for reading them.

For example, a couple of years ago, John found himself lucky enough to acquire one of the world's preeminent Franz Kafka collections from a collector named Breon Mitchell. Well, perhaps lucky is not exactly the right word.

"I had known Breon for a number of years—he'd been a customer of mine. The collection was in a bank vault in Bloomington, Indiana. I knew Breon was going to sell it at some point and when I talked to him, he told me he was just about to consign the collection to an ancient and respected British firm. I said, 'Why don't you sell it to me instead?' and I gave him what he wanted to get from the consigned sale and got the collection."

The collection consisted of over 350 books, manuscripts, translations, and critical appraisals. There were a number of presentation copies, including a plethora of first editions, most with scarce and beautiful dust jackets. If John sold all the items listed, he would have taken in something over a half-million dollars. (That's gross receipts, of course. He didn't say what he had paid for it.)

In order to announce such an extraordinary collection, John decided that the catalog should be its equal and John is nothing if not single-minded.

"That catalog almost ruined my business," he said. "I worked on it for six months. My assistant had worked on it for three months before that."

What he ended up with was eighty-three pages of text plus sixteen pages of color photographs of covers, dust jackets, manuscript pages, and printed type. The cover was black matte with "Franz Kafka" printed across the top. The "k" was lowercase, as if blown up from a typed impression. There was a period after the title, and "Lame Duck Books" was printed underneath. On the back was the Lame Duck logo, a bird with a bandaged foot, a crutch under one wing, and an open book in the other. On the inside cover it said that the collection was being offered jointly by Lame Duck, Ken Lopez Bookseller, and Between the Covers Rare Books, although the other two dealers had been listed as something of a courtesy.

"We had been kind of informal partners," John said, "and this catalog was the last gasp of that."

The first page of the catalog displayed a number of quotes both by and about Kafka, in English and German, including this one by Vladimir Nabokov:

"He is the greatest German writer of our time. Such poets as Rilke or such novelists as Mann are dwarfs or plaster saints in comparison to him."

Next was a short introduction by Breon Mitchell entitled "Collecting Kafka," in which he noted, "My goal eventually became immodest: to assemble the best collection in the world of the works of Kafka published during his lifetime." He added, "Although

Kafka, whose prose seemed a paradoxical combination of complexity and spare asceticism, was scarcely a writer one would expect to find in luxury editions . . . the physical quality of the books and periodicals published during his lifetime proved a surprise."

The photographs bear this out. Kafka's first published work was in a richly bound periodical called *Hyperion,* of which fifty numbered copies were printed on Japanese vellum. Other periodicals that published Kafka were also opulent and oversized, and Kafka's own first book was printed, at the author's insistence, in the largest available type so that the words on each page would be given the weight of poetry. Even in regular trade editions, Kafka's books, many of which came out in the war years, often featured vaguely expressionist dust jacket art, anticipating a movement that would not reach fruition until about ten years later.

After Breon Mitchell's two-page introduction, John wrote one a good deal more extensive—as fine an exposition of Kafka's genius and place in literature as will be found anywhere. The descriptions and bibliographic notes about the works themselves are equally exhaustive, at times running to a full page or even two pages for a single item.

In the end, of course, the Lame Duck Kafka catalog becomes, in itself, a legitimate bibliographic work, something that far transcends its main purpose as a sales document. Although the Kafka stands alone, John often produces catalogs, such as "Modern Thought," that straddle the line between commerce and philosophy.

Although John Wronoski has been called "one of the most important book dealers of our generation" by some of his peers, many other booksellers do not share John's philosophy of cataloging. In fact, many booksellers do not share John's philosophy of just about anything. In the very same ABAA newsletter in which John Crichton's article about the Kenneth Anderson affair appeared, there was the following from another New England dealer in "Letters to the Editor":

John Wronoski's ponderous and mannered essay [in a
previous issue] . . . made me perk up my ears and cock my
head, just like my dog used to when I'd tell her something
too complex for her limited intellect. So Wronoski's pro-
nouncements left me feeling I'd been told something
VERY important, but a little too steep for me to grasp.

Is the Internet changing the book business? Are we
lacking a training ground for younger booksellers? Has the
burgeoning trade in modern firsts altered the way we go
about our business? None of these are fresh observations,
but they are trotted out, all felicitously phrased, to support
a grander, subtler truth.

I think he wants us to read the damned things before
we sell them.

No dealer—not even John—reads every book he or she sells, of
course, but most dealers we've run into do have a surprising breadth
of knowledge about the content and not just the bibliography of
many of the books they sell. Still, John's scholarly approach to his
stock is unusual among booksellers, and he wants to make sure that
is communicated to both present and potential customers.

"I also believe that catalogs have much more than an immedi-
ate commercial function—they convey a sense of my business. I'm
creating them not just for my current customers. I'd like young
scholars to see them—people who perhaps have no idea that these
books exist, or at least certainly no idea that they are bought and
sold at these prices. In the long run, I hope this will help me locate
good customers, people who understand what my business is about.
So, I suppose catalogs become a kind of fingerprint."

The problem, of course, is that catalogs are fast becoming an en-
dangered species. A number of dealers have stopped producing
them altogether. "It's a lot of work and a big expense," said one.
"Now that any dealer can list all of his stock on the Internet,

I'm not sure why anyone would go to the trouble of producing a catalog."

The Internet certainly provides a persuasive argument against printed catalogs. In addition to saving all that time for layout and the costs of printing and postage, a dealer can update his stock (and prices) instantly and never have to worry that his listings have become dated. Moreover, dealers can get far wider dissemination of their books through the search services and a home page than they could ever hope to achieve by traditional catalog distribution. Still, as we look into the future and realize that fewer and fewer catalogs will be coming our way, we wonder how we'll ever find out about something like Michael Ondaatje's wall calendar again.

The Internet has changed more than cataloging, of course. In *Slightly Chipped,* we included a chapter on what was then the new phenomenon of on-line used-book buying that turned out to evoke more discussion than anything else in the book. (Our night at the Edgar Awards came in a close second.) We contended that, among other things, overuse of the Internet by both dealers and book lovers could, in the long run, threaten the survival of many of the very types of bookshops that bring new people into the world of used and rare books. If this business, which owes its survival to the sensory nature of the interaction of human and book, turned into one of impersonal convenience, few except those who were already attracted to the pursuit would take it up.

We didn't get a lot of agreement with this argument, particularly among dealers. Dealers *love* the Internet. Virtually every dealer we've spoken to has told us that the Internet has increased his or her business, sometimes by as much as 60 or 70 percent. What's more, Jack Borhman is not alone in utilizing the Internet as a means of acquiring books for stock—it seems that every time we've gone into Brick Walk to see Kevin Rita, he's had the eBay screen up. (Of course, he's selling through eBay too.) The one or two dealers who did agree with us about the pitfalls of on-line book collecting did so only because they were in the process of closing their shops and going exclusively cyber—the new economics had made it impossible for them to maintain a physical place of business.

What no one will deny (not even us) is that the Internet has irrevocably altered what was previously a rarefied and cloistered industry.

"The ultimate effect," said John Wronoski, "will be to create a lot more book people, but in the short run, what on-line bookselling has actually created is a lot of second-order dealers. There is no question that there has been a loss of tactility—even an illiterate bookseller can walk into a room and pick out the best book and you can't very well do that off a computer screen. Also, with these second-order dealers, there is a lot of, for want of a better word, plagiarism. They use terms without really knowing what they mean, so their customers won't know either.

"Selling on-line is not a big part of my own business," John went on, "but it's enough so that it probably makes up for the business I've lost because of the Internet."

Although dealers sell through their own Web sites, an overwhelming percentage of cyber-selling is done through the search engines, usually listing services in which a potential customer can search by title, author, or keyword, with subpasses for edition, presence of a dust jacket, or even signed copies. In *Slightly Chipped,* we mentioned the four search services that existed at that time. They were Advanced Book Exchange (ABE), Bibliocity, Bibliofind, and Interloc. We said that by the time people read that chapter, the nature of these services might well have changed.

At least we were right about something.

All four of the services had been started in a kind of mom-and-pop fashion. Interloc was begun by Richard Weatherford as a listing service for dealers, the other three as places where dealers could list books and offer them directly to the public. (There was a fifth service, Bookfinder, which was merely a superlisting, combining the listings of all four of the other search engines on one page. Then, as now, there was an enormous amount of repetition since most dealers listed with at least two services, often more.)

All four services thrived. Bibliofind, for example, went from nothing to over nine million books in only three or four years. More than that, as book buyers could view every dealer who was selling a book that he or she wanted, prices were probably forced down. Internet business was so good, in fact, that, as we noted, more than a few dealers closed their shops entirely and operated strictly on-line. Still others, who had never opened a shop at all and would never have considered doing so, became the kind of instant dealers that John Wronoski had warned against. The services these dealers listed through made it plain that they in no way could be held responsible for the accuracy of anything posted. Those who maintained physical premises saw a greater and greater percentage of their business shift to e-commerce, which in turn increased their reliance on both the listing services and their own Web pages, which by now almost every dealer had developed.

In February 1999, *Forbes* reported on "sellers of used, rare, and out-of-print books [who were] cashing in on the Internet." *Forbes* called these dealers "baby Amazons," and described the experience of one Rhode Island dealer who closed her shop after twelve years to operate strictly on-line. Soon thereafter, she had the fortuitous experience of going to bed one night only to wake up in the morning with one thousand dollars in new sales.

There were, of course, the inevitable foul-ups too. Books were delivered late or not at all, leaving the buyer to try and get his money back from someone who might not even live in the same country. Much more common were books whose condition had been described optimistically, where "near fine" actually meant nearly falling apart. We bought a first edition of *The River* by Rumer Godden, only to find that a number of pages had been stitched in upside down. We buy very few books off the Internet and make it a practice to telephone the dealer before we order anything. In this case, even after such a call, we found that the book was in a condition such that we would never have bought it had we seen it first.

As usual, Dick Weatherford at Interloc figured out a way to turn problems into revenue. His plan, as we noted in *Slightly Chipped,* was to add verification and guaranteed shipping to his service. He opened a warehouse to which every book purchased from his newly named Alibris would be shipped from a member dealer before being forwarded to the customer. Before final shipment, the books were examined and repackaged. Those that were not as advertised were returned before the customer incurred any charge. If the dealer couldn't deliver the book in a timely fashion, the customer could cancel the transaction. Originally, his plan was to cover the cost of all of this by requiring member dealers to give him the standard 20 percent dealer discount—a discount which, of course, would not be passed on to the customer.

Also as usual, Dick added a couple of wrinkles. First of all, a book listed on Alibris lacked any mention of the dealer who was actually selling it. Alibris was Alibris and that was that. Also, when the book arrived at the customer's address, it came from Alibris, not the dealer. In addition, when the customer ordered off Alibris, he or she was ordering from the service, not the dealer. In other words, if you were a dealer listing on Alibris, you lost all ability to communicate with the customer buying your book. You couldn't add him or her to your mailing list, send e-mails, or try to find out if there was anything else in your stock that this collector might want. The customer, in turn, had no idea which dealer he had just purchased from, and thus could not establish a relationship where future purchases might be done directly.

This became even more important because Alibris didn't simply cover its additional costs through the dealer discount. They marked up the price to the customer as well, thus collecting on both ends of the transaction. If a dealer got an Alibris order for a book that he or she was selling for $50, it was instantly marked down to $40, but Alibris might collect $60 or $65. By keeping buyer and seller apart, Alibris prevented them from cutting out what had become an expensive middleman on future sales.

"We're a dealer, not a classified ad service," Dick Weatherford insisted. "Do you know any other dealers who tell a customer, 'Oh, I bought this from a dealer down the street before I sold it to you. Here's his name.'? And don't you think when one dealer buys from another dealer, they mark up the price before they sell it to a customer? That's all we do. Every book we sell passes through our warehouse and is shipped by our personnel. More than that, we own about one million books outright."

Neither higher prices nor uncertain transactions made a dent in the e-commerce tidal wave and all the search engines thrived. This success brought about the inevitable result—used books began to attract the attention of the big boys, Amazon and Barnes & Noble.

Amazon had already been selling out-of-print books on a search basis. Even though they were marking these searches up by a huge percentage, something as labor-intensive as searching for a one-of-a-kind item whose price often would not exceed one hundred dollars did not represent a profitable allocation of their resources.

Amazon and Barnes & Noble realized that the easiest way to overcome the diseconomies of scale inherent in dealing with the out-of-print market piecemeal was to buy up the whole thing, or at least enough of it to give them a large enough gross profit to justify being in the business. The best place to find these oversized chunks of the business were, of course, the search engines, which had done all that aggregating already. Now, less than two years after we wrote about the Internet in *Slightly Chipped,* not one of the four search engines still exists in the form it did then.

The first to go was ABE. In a move that was furiously criticized at the time, but that now seems tame, ABE sold a minority share of its business to barnesandnoble.com. In return, in addition to lots of money, ABE gained the right to have its books listed on the barnesandnoble.com Web site. It is still unclear which side initiated this deal, but it was the first time that the out-of-print and in-print markets had been merged in a serious way.

It wasn't that the owners of the other search engines didn't realize that they were sitting on ready-made plug-ins to the major on-line booksellers—it was simply that, until the ABE deal, the traditional independence of sellers of used and antiquarian books had carried over to the on-line market.

After ABE, that all changed. The next to go was Bibliofind. As we also noted in *Slightly Chipped,* one of the two founders of Bibliofind, Michael Selzer, had been vociferous (to say the least) in his condemnation of the ABE/barnesandnoble.com deal. He sent an e-mail to all ABE member booksellers (who were, by and large, also his booksellers) claiming that he had been approached first, but had turned down barnesandnoble.com on moral grounds, and that the ABE deal could quite possibly be the beginning of the end for all of them. By implication, of course, he was saying that never, ever, would he sell out like that.

Then, less than one year later, in January 1999, along comes e-Niche, a high-powered on-line development group based in Cambridge, Massachusetts, which buys out Bibliofind lock, stock, and Selzers for an undisclosed sum rumored to be above seven figures. Michael Selzer claimed e-Niche's offer was the first that showed a concern for "preserving the values of antiquarian bookselling." Conspicuous by their absence on a post-acquisition advisory board filled with venture capitalists was anyone in the book business in general and anyone named Selzer in particular.

Only four months after that, e-Niche, which had changed its name to Exchange.com, bundled Bibliofind with a similar search engine for music, then turned around and sold the package to Amazon.com. Exchange.com was part of a three-company purchase announced by Amazon that day, so no one knows the exact selling price, although Exchange.com was generally considered the most important of the three, and Bibliofind was the most important part of Exchange.com. The price for all three: $645 million in Amazon.com stock. (Not anymore, of course.)

The Bibliofind deal notwithstanding, without question the most aggressive company in the field of used and antiquarian books remains, of course, Alibris.

In April 2000, Alibris announced that they had secured $30 million in funding from a consortium of venture capital firms including CMGI@Ventures (a NASDAQ-100 company) and Ingram Book Group. This brought their total funding, according to the *New York Times,* to over $60 million.

Alibris's plans for the money are even more ambitious. They have announced an advertising campaign of up to $100 million. Already, big, splashy, full-color ads have regularly appeared in such publications as the *New York Times Book Review,* the *New Yorker, Harper's, Smithsonian* magazine, *Gourmet,* and *Vanity Fair,* featuring images of covers of books like *Instant Replay* by Green Bay Packer Hall of Fame guard Jerry Kramer, *Steal This Book* by Abbie Hoffman, and *On the Road* by Jack Kerouac, along with the slogan "Books You Thought You'd Never Find." The idea, according to the company, is "to illustrate the idea of rediscovering special books, like your first childhood book or your grandmother's favorite cookbook."

"We don't advertise in *Firsts* or *AB Bookman's Weekly* or *Book* magazine," said Dick Weatherford, now chairman of the new Alibris. "We're not interested in the collector market at all. We think that collectors are well served by existing trade channels. We're after a more general group. I was at my optometrist's the other day when he happened to say, 'I've been looking for this book.' It was out-of-print so I told him to check Alibris."

This is the first time that a used-book concern has made a serious commitment to breaking out of the small collectors' circle and into the mainstream (a market that is also, of course, far more naïve about pricing and condition) but the general book-loving consumer market is only a part of the plan.

"Most of our sales are business to business. For example, it costs a library between forty and forty-five dollars to set up a vendor relationship. If a library is adding to its collection and wants books that are out of print, that's forty or forty-five dollars for each used-book dealer. They're happy to pay a markup to us in order to consolidate their business and only have to deal with one vendor. We fill orders for hundreds of books at a time. A library can save thousands of dollars on a transaction like that. We have other types of relationships where we can fill large orders too."

They sure have. In perhaps its most strategic move yet, Alibris made a deal with barnesandnoble.com to list its books on the Barnes & Noble out-of-print page. Now, if you'll remember, Barnes & Noble had previously bought a chunk of ABE specifically in order to list *their* books. The deal with Alibris, however, specified that Alibris's listings would be first; that is, ahead of ABE's. Needless to say ABE was not pleased, but lacked enough clout to make a stink. In an interview, Kathy Waters of ABE said, "We weren't happy about it but we continue to maintain a very strong working relationship with Barnes and Noble."

Sure. Just like Ivana Trump maintained a strong working relationship with The Donald after she got dumped for the younger and sleeker Marla.

But if ABE is unhappy now, there might be more surprises on the horizon. In a *New York Times* article, Alibris CEO Martin Manley hinted that Alibris was considering swallowing up ABE as well.

When asked about this a few weeks later, Dick Weatherford said, "We have no plans at all to buy ABE." However, after we mentioned that *Warmly Inscribed* would not be published for a year, Dick joked, "Oh, we'll probably own ABE by then."

They already own Bibliocity. Alibris bought the Australian-based search engine, which had specialized in rare, high-end antiquarian books, in October 1999. The acquisition both broadened the Alibris inventory base and eliminated a competitor.

"That's not the reason we did it, though," said Dick Weatherford. "The two brothers who owned Bibliocity are brilliant programmers. You just can't find people like that. We acquired the company as much to access their skills as for any other reason."

We asked if it was difficult to conduct a relationship, even a cyber-relationship, with two people who lived halfway around the world.

"Oh, they moved here," said Dick. "They live in the San Francisco area now."

There have been a number of new search services that have sprung up in the wake of all this, but Dick says that Alibris has no interest.

"I think many of these services started because they hope to be bought out, but that's not going to happen. There's simply no need. Besides, the small dealers that they bring on just don't add anything."

Alibris has been everywhere. The month before the Bibliocity acquisition, the company made a deal with eBay to provide rare and antiquarian books for auction in eBay Great Collections, the on-line auction company's new category devoted to "authenticated art and collectibles." There have been deals with Ingram, the book distributor (already an investor), to list out-of-print books on Ingram's new "I-Page," a subscription stock inquiry and order-entry service.

Not surprisingly, with the exception of Dick Weatherford, the management of Alibris reads much more like Wall Street than book street. The company is very proud of its management team and on its Web site gives full backgrounds, along with color pictures, of the thirteen most senior people in the organization. Other than Dick, not one of them has a day of experience in the used- and rare-book trade, and only one other manager has any experience in books at all. On the other hand, as the past few years have shown us, you don't really need people who know an issue point from needlepoint in order to float a successful IPO.

In order to see how all this razzle-dazzle finance has affected prices, on April 18, 2000, we conducted an experiment. We decided to choose a book at random, and then compare the prices as we found them on the various search engines. We hoped to be able to compare the same book from the same dealers in order to see how prices varied from one source to another.

The book we chose at random was a terrific little volume entitled *Used and Rare: Travels in the Book World*. It's by a husband-and-wife writing team and is universally considered a super read. (The authors are said to be charming and youthful too.)

In any event, we first called up ABE. Among the listings for *Used and Rare* was a first edition from Horizon West Books for $45 (book fine/dust jacket fine), a first from Black Dog Books also for $45 (near fine/fine), a third from D. Brooke & Son for $50 (as new/as new), a first from Leather Stalking Books for $55 (fine/fine), a third from A. R. Backer Books for $25 (fine/fine), and a fourth from The General's Aid for $45 (as new/fine).

Next was Bibliofind. We found the exact same listings at the same prices for Leather Stalking Books, Horizon West, D. Brooke & Son, Black Dog, The General's Aide, Backer, and a number of other listings.

After that, things got interesting. We called up barnesandnoble. com and went to their used and out-of-print inventory. Guess what? The Leather Stalking Books copy was there too, only now it was $79.95. Horizon West was there too, at the bargain price of $65.25. The General's Aide was also $65.25, as was Black Dog. A. R. Backer was $40. Except for the price, everything else in the book description was *exactly the same*. Barnes and Noble was selling books that anyone could buy on two other free and readily accessible search engines for up to 60 percent more.

As noted, Alibris is slicker, not identifying the dealers whose books they are selling. Instead, they merely list title, edition, condition, and price. Still, there are clues. For example, there is one listing that states, "1st (stated) 4th printing . . ." (this is a fourth, not at all a first, by the way) "AS NEW/FINE minor dj rubbing." The price is $56. This is the same exact description as that for the $45 book offered by The General's Aide on both ABE and Bibliofind and for $65.25 on bandn.com. Thus, Alibris is marking up a $45 book by only 25 percent instead of the almost 50 percent that bandn.com is trying to get away with.

According to their agreement, Barnes & Noble is now listing for Alibris. A few weeks after the initial experiment we ran a follow-up to see if bandn.com is marking up the already marked-up Alibris prices. What do you think we found? In the *Used and Rare* listings, this time for a paperback, under the description "New Book, Very good condition LOC Call No: 98-014332, [Goldstone, Lawrence Born: 1947], p. cm. Trade Softcover," Alibris was listing the book for $17. For a book of the exact same description, bandn.com was charging $23.50. (Of course, *Used and Rare* is available in softcover through regular channels for the cover price of $11.95.)

What this little test demonstrates is that the further a buyer is removed from a dealer, the more he or she has to pay. At present, of course, a savvy book buyer can access all three (or four) levels of price and choose the one that suits most—a choice that we hope is obvious. But the only places left for the buyer to get any sort of deal at all are on the remaining undigested (although not necessarily unacquired) search engines, ABE or Bibliofind, or those new search engines, like BookAvenue, that, according to Dick Weatherford, are only waiting to be bought out anyway. When those go, and there is every reason to think they will, a book buyer may end up having no direct access to a dealer at all. Then, all this multiple listing, worldwide access, and competition that was supposed to drive down prices will have had exactly the opposite effect.

On the other hand, Dick Weatherford may well make more money from selling used or rare books than any other man in history.

Chapter 6

BOOKING THE TREND

A frequent topic of conversation in the book world is the passing of the independent bookstore. We actually came across two that are opening.

We found the first on an afternoon when we had gone into Manhattan to visit the Metropolitan Museum of Art. We had just finished Michael Frayn's excellent comic novel *Headlong,* which is about the possible discovery of a lost Brueghel, and we wanted to see the only one of the Seasons series that is not in a museum in Europe. After we were done, we decided to head over to Madison Avenue and visit the Burlington Book Shop. When we got to the location, there was still a bookshop there, but it certainly wasn't Burlington.

The shop was now called Crawford Doyle and, although the basic layout was the same, the differences from Burlington were immediately apparent. First of all, the place was light. Even though there were large windows on both sides of the front door that faced out onto Madison Avenue, Burlington had always exuded that dingy, catacomblike quality much more common to a used-book store. In fact, Burlington had been part used-book store. A man named Ari

Megiddo leased a tight, narrow, impossibly hot balcony that over-looked the main selling floor. The bookcases were in a space so cramped that you literally had to lie on the floor in order to see the books on the lower shelves. On top of that (or more accurately, on the bottom), the books were doubled so that, unless you liked to play those tile puzzle games, you couldn't possibly manage to see everything. (We were later told that there were an additional ten thousand books in the basement.)

Ari specialized in good used books and, climatic conditions notwithstanding, we had frequently found things we wanted and the prices, especially for Madison Avenue, had not been exorbitant. We got a very nice first edition of *The Wall* by John Hersey, for example, for twenty-five dollars.

One advantage of Ari's area was that when the employees gossiped about the publishing industry—which they did regularly—we could inevitably pick up some choice item about who had been fired, who had changed houses, and what books were going to be pushed in the coming season. We never really figured out how people lurking in what amounted to a glorified aisle came by all this information, but it always turned out to be accurate. The last time we were there, Ari's staff was all aflutter about a then-upcoming reissue of a self-published book entitled *Give Me My Father's Body*. It was about a group of Eskimos who were brought to New York at the end of the nineteenth century and housed in the basement of the American Museum of Natural History, where all except one child, a boy named Minik, died miserable and lonely deaths. Minik, they said, was later put up for adoption and told that his father's remains were being shipped home for a tribal burial. What the museum really did was stuff him or something and put him out on display. Ari's crew was talking about how the film rights had just been bought by Kevin Spacey and how, as a result, the book was going to be BIG. The museum, they went on, was not going to cooperate in the film production. About three months later, we read an article in *Publishers Weekly* that said much the same thing as we had learned eavesdropping at Ari's.

While Ari's garret remained unchanged in the new Crawford Doyle, the main floor had been altered considerably. There was a crisp, clean look to the place, the old Burlington shelves had been replaced with stained mahogany or cherry, and the cash register had been moved to the side to open up the center of the store. Now, even though floor space was limited, you could move around and browse comfortably.

More than that, out-of-print books were no longer confined to the second floor. In a glass-enclosed display case just behind the cash register were featured a number of modern firsts—not Ari's used books, but high-end collector stuff that Crawford Doyle itself was selling. There was a copy of Robert Owen Butler's surprise Pulitzer Prize–winning *A Good Scent from a Strange Mountain* for $200, *Ratner's Star* by Don DeLillo for $250, and a very nice copy of *On the Road* for $3,600. Without exception, the prices might generously be described as aggressive but, considering this was one of the most expensive neighborhoods in Manhattan, they obviously were not inappropriate to the local clientele.

"Yes, this was Burlington before," confirmed the woman behind the desk. Her name was Dot and she had white hair and outstanding posture. "It was bought a couple of years ago by a couple, Judy Crawford and John Doyle. Judy did the design for the store. John used to work for IBM."

"I worked for IBM for thirty-six years," said John Doyle, a thin, quiet man with gray hair and a gray beard. He was wearing a pale red plaid button-down shirt with no tie. His wife, Judy, was beautiful and Southern-elegant, with long gray hair tied back and a maroon blouse. We met them for lunch at a little country French place down the street. "I sold typewriters to start out. Later, I was in management. I had executive jobs all over the world. At my last job we lived in Japan—I was in charge of leasing operations in Asia.

"It's easy to keep working. You're making more than you're worth and your pension's going up every year. But I was getting close to sixty and IBM is a young man's company. I didn't want to get pushed out. It's humiliating. So I told them I was retiring.

"I started looking around for something else to do and thought about a bookstore. I love books, I didn't need to make money, and a bookstore didn't need much capital.

"So, after I retired, I went to bookseller's school. The ABA sponsors it. I went to one in Washington for a week and it was very helpful. After that, I volunteered at bookstores for about a year to learn the business. I worked here, at Burlington, but the woman who owned the store was broke and she couldn't buy any more books, so I had to go to another store—Verso, on Eighth Avenue and Fifteenth Street—to learn that end of the business. It's very humbling to enter a new field. At first you don't know anything and you have to get started at the beginning. I began by shelving books.

"In the meantime, I got to know the landlord here. He eventually got frustrated with the woman and kicked her out and Judy and I took the space. We gutted it for two or three months, then fixed it up and reopened. That was five years ago.

"It was kind of fun—what's interesting is inventing something, some process, learning something new. The hardest thing is to build the inventory. I took the fiction list from Verso—they got it from Wordsmith in Boston—and Dot developed the biography section. You have to buy inventory. You can return it, but only for credit. We buy mostly from publishers. I don't like Ingram or Baker and Taylor; they're just processors. I like working with the publishers and their reps and going to the parties.

"The biggest issue for us is quality. We learned this from the Japanese at IBM. Customers don't expect more, but they certainly don't expect less.

"Of course, we were the beneficiaries of sixty years of Burlington. And, anyway, the key to the independent book business is location. Our store is on the way to the Met. Thousands of people walk down Madison Avenue right by our store every week. A lot of them are tourists. The tourists buy books from us that they could buy at home. But they say, 'We don't have time when we're working to buy books,' so while they're here on vacation they buy from us.

"We're also lucky because so many authors live around here, and are customers. Tom Wolfe—he lives right around the corner. William Goldman stops in, William Boyd. A. S. Byatt loves paperweights and the best paperweight store in New York is right next door so she always stops in afterwards. We have historians, biographers. . . ."

We asked about Dot, the woman we had spoken to on our previous visit. She had been vibrant, funny, and helpful. We seemed to remember that she had been part of the Burlington staff as well.

"Oh yes," John replied. "If Dot left, we'd have to close—people call her from all over the world—London, Paris—to buy books."

"So how has it gone?" we asked. "Everyone tells us that an independent bookstore can't make money anymore."

"The biggest problem in the book business is the margin," said John. "A book sells for thirteen dollars, and we get it for around eight. Basically, you're sitting with one hundred thousand books at a forty percent margin—it's not enough. There's rent, remember—it's one hundred thousand dollars a year here. I don't think that this store could ever be profitable. When you take into account that Judy and I work for nothing . . .

"At our store, if we sell three copies of a book, that's good," he added.

We asked how big a part of the business the first-edition side was and if Ari minded the competition.

"We don't really compete," John said. "We aim at a different market. The only reason he's here at all, I think, is that it's a terrific place to get hold of lots of books when people decide to get rid of them for one reason or another.

"As for us, the out-of-print books are probably no more than ten percent of our business ordinarily. Of course, we also help people build libraries. This one fellow came in—he'd never read fiction and he wanted to start a library and he wanted fiction. He said he wanted to collect all the good fiction since World War Two. 'I want to get all the Saul Bellow, the Philip Roth,' he said. In other words, all the books by a given author.

"So I said, 'That's dumb, most of the books they've written aren't very good.' And he let us develop a list of like eight or nine hundred books published since World War Two and then he said, 'Okay, go get them.'

"We got almost everything for under five hundred dollars—there were only a few over a thousand, like *Catcher in the Rye.*"

John paused. "That one fellow skewed our sales quite a bit. Of course this guy—typical—has since lost interest and is off buying stocks on the Internet."

We found the second new store quite by accident, when, one day, Nancy's grandmother Ruth called.

You might remember Ruth. She is the widow of Clarence Wolf, who helped start us on our book journey way back in *Used and Rare.* Ruth is now well into her nineties and going strong. She still lives in the immaculate apartment in Chicago surrounded by objets d'art and books. She puts on large picture hats to go out to lunch and maintains a strong interest in the stock market. It is only by strenuous efforts on the part of the rest of the family that she is dissuaded from day trading.

"Hello, Grandma Ruth, how are you?"

"I'm fine, dear. I had a phone call I wanted to tell you about. I spoke to Doug Phillips today. He was our insurance agent for many years. Do you remember him? He called when your first book came out and said he didn't know Clarence was a collector. Apparently, Doug is a collector, too. He tried several times to come over and see Clarence's books while he was still alive, but something always came up. Anyway, do you know what he's done? He's resigned from the insurance business! He's going to open an antiquarian bookstore in

Chicago. He's calling it Printers Row Fine and Rare Books. I believe he's trying for a June opening."

"Really. That's very interesting."

"I have his telephone number here. You know, he spoke very
highly of your book to Clarence. He was a very nice young man."

"Well, maybe we'll call him. It's an interesting decision—to quit
your job to open a bookstore."

"It certainly is!" said Ruth. "Of course, he's lucky he didn't go
into the market. It's losing value, you know."

"Bad day?"

"Terrible. I may have to sell some of my shares tomorrow. I
don't like the way things look." She sighed. "When I think where I
should have sold . . . Of course, it may come back. . . ."

"I've been a collector since the late 1970s, early 1980s," said Doug
Phillips when we got him on the phone. "I've always loved books,
but it's really been the last fifteen years that I've immersed myself in
them. I'm embarrassed to admit this, but I started collecting when I
got a mailing from some first-edition club. They weren't real first
editions; they were replicas, kind of like Folio Society or Easton
Press, that kind of book, but then I thought what a great thing it
would be to have the originals. The original first edition of *The
Great Gatsby,* the original Twain, Dickens, Henry James, Edith
Wharton—I'm a nineteenth-century literature sort of person, although of course there are great twentieth-century authors I want
as well.

"Then I read the biography of A. S. W. Rosenbach and that
inspired me. I realized it was my dream to have a really great bookstore. A bookstore like Rosenbach had—like Heritage in Los Angeles or Bauman's in New York. That kind of bookstore.

"Of course, Chicago has always had great bookstores. When I
was growing up, there was Main Street Bookstore on Michigan
Avenue. I remember Mrs. Vandermark worked there. She wore her

hair in a bun with some kind of chopsticks in it. Every day after school I would go and sort of hang out there and she was so nice.

"Main Street was a new bookstore, but they would order anti-quarian books for you if you asked. When I was eleven, I saw *The King and I* and I wanted to read the original source book. Mrs. Van-dermark ordered it for me from an English bookstore. It was called *The English Governess at the Siamese Court: Being Recollections of Six Years in the Royal Palace at Bangkok* and it was written by Anna Har-riette Leonowens.

"All these years I was your grandparents' insurance agent and I never knew that your grandfather was a book collector. Then my dad died and I sold my interest in the business to my brother. I'm forty-three years old—I was forty-one when I made the decision to open a store. I went looking along Printers Row and fell in love with a space—it's a storefront. Now I'm remodeling. It's going to look like an old English bookstore, you know, with a library ladder and even a place for tea. I went looking at other bookstores for de-sign ideas and when I went into Prairie Avenue Books, which has books about design and architecture, I said to myself, I want who-ever designed this store to design mine. It turned out the owner had designed it—he's a prominent architect—and I hired him.

"I'm going to have my preview opening at the Printers Row Book Fair," said Doug.

"What's the Printers Row Book Fair?"

"It's this really big book fair in Chicago—they had seventy thousand people last year. It coincides with a music festival. In addi-tion, Mayor Daley has just created the Greater Loop Book District, listing all the bookshops in downtown Chicago. There's a brochure with a map. I'll send you one. Anyway, the fair is really something. Even if the store isn't totally finished, I'm going to have books in the window so people can see what I've got."

"What have you got? Where did you get your books?"

"Oh, I've been going all over the country buying books for

years now. I've got over ten thousand books. A lot of them are in the attic. I've got a huge attic," he said. "My original plan was to just operate an Internet business out of my house, but I really, really wanted an open store. Everyone said, 'You're crazy! Don't open a store.' You know, they say things like, 'If you want to become a millionaire as a bookseller, start with two million'—that kind of thing. But I'm excited.

"Of course, I really love my books. It's going to be hard to part with them."

"What do you have?"

"I've got a Shakespeare Second Folio; that's probably my most special book. I've got some unusual things, too. I was at an auction and they had a *Great Gatsby* and I bought it. A lot of people know about the issue point in the text, which says 'sick in tired' instead of 'sickantired' but there's an issue point on the dust jacket, too, that's much less well known. In about the first hundred books printed, the first letter of Jay Gatsby's name was printed with a lowercase 'j' instead of a capital. Instead of reprinting it, Scribners actually got a calligrapher to come in and go over all those books and make the 'j' a capital. But you can still see where the lower case 'j' had been. When I bought the book, it turned out to be a first state even though it wasn't sold as one. That's probably the best accident that's ever happened to me. It's going to be especially hard to sell those things.

"Why don't you come to the Printers Row Book Fair?" he suggested. "It's June third and fourth. It sounds right up your alley."

The Printers Row Book Fair was the brainchild of the Near South Planning Board, a neighborhood community-development organization, and was begun sixteen years ago as a way to attract visitors to a seedy, almost abandoned part of the South Loop, which a few hearty urban homesteaders were then trying to reclaim. In fact, State Street, only one block over from Dearborn, on which the fair is held, was Chicago's skid row and the Mission is still there.

Now, however, with gentrification in full flower, the fair has evolved into a celebration of the success of that effort and of an historic district's renewed vitality. Huge office buildings are being converted into luxury apartments and condominiums; there are upscale retail shops and eateries all along Dearborn, including the trendy, high-priced Printers Row Restaurant. "It's hot. It's an unbelievably hot area," said Mary Davis Fournier, the fair's organizer. "The mayor lives here."

At the south end of the fair is the renovated, red-brick Dearborn Station, now the home of a bank and a brokerage house, among other outlets. Here the preeminent African-American historian John Hope Franklin was to offer a kickoff speech at eleven on Saturday morning. Periodically throughout the day, there would be an announcement over the speaker system of a free bus tour through the district so that visitors could see all the new housing and businesses that were under development.

In the sixteen years, the fair has grown from a neighborhood event to the largest literary festival in the Midwest, now attracting over 160 booksellers from all over the area. Most of the exhibitors were set up in large white tents that had been placed in the center of Dearborn Avenue running from Congress Parkway three blocks down to Dearborn Station. There was also a tent devoted to storytelling and children's literature and another to around-the-clock poetry readings. The Chicago Public Library, the main branch of which was a block or two away, had set up a tent where staffers were encouraging passersby to sign up for library cards. Jugglers, clowns, and storybook characters walked among the crowd, and music was piped in. Balloons bounced in the wind and there were lots of food stalls.

This was really a street fair that happened to be devoted to books; unpretentious, creative, and buoyant—pure Chicago, the city at its best, the side of its personality that has produced deep-dish pizza, hot little jazz clubs, and the Steppenwolf Theater Company. And, just to make sure that fair-goers got that full Chicago flavor, the legendary breeze whipped in off Lake Michigan, turning a calm, sunny, seventy-degree June day into a wind-chilled, sunny, forty-degree June day. We were not the only people underdressed for the conditions. There were so many goose-bumped bare legs that it looked like a plucked drumstick convention.

Even at ten o'clock in the morning, when the fair had just opened, the booths and sidewalks were filled with browsers. The crowd was remarkably young and diverse for a book fair. There were a number of couples who seemed to be there on dates. Lots of children as well. Dogs too. Still, it was all completely orderly and everyone showed great respect for the books.

Then there was the tall, burly Chicago police sergeant with the red, thinning hair. He was dressed in full uniform, including an impressive-looking sidearm, and was carrying a light blue riot helmet under one arm. He was going from booth to booth, perusing the stock, often pulling out books to look them over. His taste seemed to run mostly to modern firsts. For example, we saw him leaf carefully through *Voyage of the Narwhal,* a feminist take on Arctic exploration.

We thought this was adorable—a big, tough Chicago police sergeant who was also a book collector. We decided to approach him, but we didn't know quite how to initiate the conversation.

"Are you browsing?" we asked stupidly.

"Yes," he snarled. "I'm browsing." He turned our way and glared. "I'm working too. If someone takes anything, I'll lock them up."

This was a little unnerving. "So you're under cover?" blurted one of us, even more stupidly, feeling suspicion fall her way.

"I'm not under cover. I'm on duty." The sergeant clearly was upset that he was too young to have been around in 1968, the good old days when he could have just cracked us over the head with a billy club.

At that point, we felt it prudent to mosey on off and take our notepad and our misplaced inquisitiveness somewhere else.

The fair was heavily weighted toward good reading copies and solid used books. There were probably only four or five dealers who were selling anything for over one hundred dollars, but there were also a number of what could generously be described as nontraditional dealers who made things fun in a way that we don't usually associate with a literary event. For example, a standard used-book dealer selling low-priced Tarzans and the Hardy Boys was right next to the plump, healthy-looking men and women of The Vegetarian Resource Group, who were extolling the virtues of meatless dining and handing out free copies of "The Vegetarian Journal," the cover of which featured an enticing photograph of "Beautiful Broccoli" and promised "6 Soothing Miso Soups" inside.

There was one booth devoted to revolutionary literature, featuring such titles as "Che Speaks to Children," and another selling banners and T-shirts bearing the message "Free Mumia," the black activist who was scheduled to be executed in Philadelphia.

We hadn't been there five minutes before we became aware with a start that this was a fair where we could afford just about everything. After years of drooling at the New York Antiquarian Book Fair, this realization left us a bit light-headed. Even better, the selection was so off-the-wall that we might find really good stuff. We immediately checked to see how much money we had brought.

Halfway down the first block was a booth that was unmarked but run by a guy from Clinton, Michigan, who called himself Out of the Way Books. Out of the Way only did fairs. Most of the books were okay but undistinguished. Then, on the top shelf at the back of the booth, we saw a copy of Somerset Maugham's *Ashenden or the British Agent*. It was a Doubleday Doran 1941 reprint. What made this book unusual was the dust jacket, which was brightly colored with a red, crouching lion, a volcano, a small Eiffel Tower, and, in the background, the figure of a man with a hat, trench coat, briefcase, and umbrella.

There is a ton of editions of *Ashenden* and it seems to be a book that lends itself to unusual dust jacket art. When we first started collecting, we saw a first edition at Peter Stern's shop in Boston with a dust jacket that had crossing beams of light against a red background. That copy was $2,500. This copy was not a first edition, of course—but the dust jacket was crisp, unusual, more attractive, and selling for $12.50.

"Good fair," noted the one with the cash.

A little way down the street was Toad Hall Books, which was located in Rockford, about eighty miles west of Chicago. They had a little frog-green brochure with an illustration of Toad from *The Wind in the Willows* on the front.

"Toad Hall is our name for pop and not-so-pop culture," said the brochure. "Toad Hall is art, music, and literature as available in a remarkable variety of forms."

True enough. Toad Hall certainly didn't limit itself to books. There were art, music, and "General Nostalgia," which included old toys and games; collectibles in paper; political buttons; TV-related items like soundtracks, guides, and stills; radio memorabilia; local history; genealogy; and baseball cards.

As for the books, Toad Hall had some titles with which we'd never come in contact before. Among them were:

BLOCK THAT KICK! Featuring a cover illustration of an old-time football player (skinny and tall instead of huge and muscled) and written by Harold M. Sherman, author of *TOUCHDOWN; The Ski Patrol* by someone named Snell; and *King of the Royal Mounted and the Ghost Guns of Roaring River* with a dust jacket featuring a cartoonlike illustration of an earnest-looking Royal Mounted Policeman in profile leaning forward on a large brown charger.

More familiarly, they also had lots of those big little books for forty or fifty dollars apiece that we saw at the Bienes Library in Fort Lauderdale.

We almost bought H. P. Lovecraft's *The Lurker at the Threshold,* which was wrapped in plastic and looked to be an original paperback, when we saw a hardcover of George Orwell's *Keep the Aspidistra Flying.* This novel had been made into a quirky British film starring Helena Bonham Carter and Richard E. Grant, which was

released in this country as *A Merry War*. It's about Gordon Com-
stock, a middle-class man who quits his job at an advertising company in early-twentieth-century Britain in order to become a famous
poet and have sex in the afternoon . . . exactly like his upper-class
publisher. The book was a first American in excellent condition for
forty dollars. What the heck.

We handed the book to a man in his twenties with red, spikey
hair and a couple of earrings. We asked if Toad Hall was his, and he
told us no, that he was here working for a woman named Beverly
who was still back in Rockford.

"But she works with him," the red-haired man went on, gesturing toward an older man in a leather jacket who was standing off
to the side.

"I'm Mean Streets," the man said when we went over. "We
have two buildings with seventeen rooms. We probably have a million pieces of memorabilia. I'm the mystery guy. I have ten thousand vintage mysteries."

"Your name isn't really Mean Streets, is it?"

He leaned forward. "I'll give you a card," he whispered. "But I
don't give it out very often. I only do big deals. I have superior vintage mysteries, like David Goodis's first book in first edition and
Raymond Chandler in first edition." He looked around, like this
was the moment he was going to hand over the drugs. "My name is
Dan," he whispered.

We asked Dan, who we surmised might have been reading from
his stock a little too much, if he came to this fair often.

"Yes," he said. "It's a very good fair. Sometimes the weather gets
you, though. Then you have to pull your books as far back under
the tent as you can and hope for the best. Also . . ." he glanced
around once more, "you have to bring enough people to watch your
books. There are a lot of light-fingered people at this fair. There was
even a woman in a wheelchair stashing books in it."

Just down from Toad Hall and Mean Streets was a booth specializing in witchcraft and the occult, with such titles as *The Ency-*

clopedia of Ancient and Forbidden Knowledge by somebody named Zolar, *Zelma the Mystic,* and *Witchcraft and the Magic of Africa.* We were tempted to buy something here as well, just for the novelty if nothing else, but we were afraid it might open up a whole new area of collecting. Besides, we might use the spells on each other when we were arguing over sentence structure. Instead, we bought Emily a Scholastic "Voyages of Discovery" book called *The History of Making Books: From Clay Tablets, Papyrus Rolls, and Illuminated Manuscripts to the Printing Press* at a booth a little farther down. There were sections on bookbinding, book burning, and the power of the press and foldouts of famous libraries. The book had an illuminated manuscript on the cover. There were a stack of them, each selling for half-price. They must have been seconds but were in perfectly good shape.

Right next to a dealer specializing in prints of old Chicago—things like the railroad strike and the old Stock Exchange—was Joyce & Company. Here, we saw a copy of an issue of the *Yellow Book,* the radical literary journal of the 1890s for which Max Beerbohm among others had written. This was the October 1895 issue and the first copy we had ever seen for sale. The *Yellow Book,* it turned out, really was a book—hardcover as opposed to magazine format. The issue featured "A Seventh-Story Heaven" by Richard Le Gallienne, "The Queen's Pleasure" by Henry Harland, and an essay written by someone who signed himself "The Yellow Dwarf," perhaps Beardsley himself. It was only twenty dollars but it was kind of beat-up so we passed. Afterwards, we realized that we probably should have bought it anyway.

One tent down from Joyce & Company was Old Main Bookshoppe, from Champaign. By this time, the fair was so crowded that it was hard to get in to see the books, but the selection was excellent, particularly the Lincoln section. There were *Mary Lincoln: A Biography of a Marriage; This was Andersonville; The Lincoln Papers; The Wartime Papers of R. E. Lee;* and *A True History of the Assassination of Abraham Lincoln and the Conspiracy of 1865.*

As we were browsing at Old Main, we saw a woman at another booth furiously waving us over. When we got there, we noticed that this woman did not have any books, but she did have a laptop.

"Hi," she said happily, "here's a free bookmark. If you sign up for PreviewPort, you have a chance to win a free e-book."

We asked what PreviewPort was.

"Oh," said the woman, "it's Web pages of all your favorite authors. It gives you their biographies, tells you about their books, and gives you ways to contact them or get their books, even if they're out of print. Here, let me show you. . . ."

She tapped some keys on her computer then grimaced. "I can't. The system's not working right now." Then she noticed the note-taking. "If you're writers yourselves, maybe you want to use us and put a Web page on our system. Then all your fans can contact you."

We were dubious. What if we put up a Web page and no one contacted us?

This possibility had not seemed to have occurred to the PreviewPort woman. "Oh yes," she went on. "It will be terrific . . . everything an author needs. You can post work on the site, recommend books by other authors you like, even create an on-line scrapbook. Then, when you have a book coming out, we can give you a launch site. Your publisher can post advance excerpts and press-kit materials. We can even do a virtual book tour, with a reading, a visit with a book group, or an on-line publication party."

An on-line publication party? Did they serve cheap, on-line white wine?

As we walked away from the PreviewPort booth, another man, also noticing the note-taking, walked up and asked, "Are you writing about this fair for a newspaper?"

"No, but my husband and I write about old books."

"What do you have, a magazine or something?" he asked.

"No, we write books about old books. Are you a dealer?"

"No. My wife and I live in Manhattan. We come to this fair

every year." His eyes narrowed. "Someone else wrote a book about old books. Christopher somebody. Do you know that book?"

"You mean *Parnassus on Wheels*? Yes, he wrote another one after that, called *The Haunted Book Shop*. I can't think of his . . . oh, yes. It was Christopher Morley."

"That's right," the man grunted, then apparently satisfied with our credentials, turned abruptly and walked away.

We got all the way to the end of the fair at Dearborn Station, where we caught part of John Hope Franklin's remarks. He spoke passionately to a large audience about how the writing of *From Slavery to Freedom: A History of African-Americans* had been the great intellectual experience of his life. The speech was being taped by what we assumed was C-SPAN, since they had a big yellow bus parked outside that said, "Book TV C-SPAN 2" in foot-high black letters on the side.

We still hadn't figured out where Doug's booth was, so we got a map and checked. He was one of the dealers who hadn't been assigned to a tent, but to a sidewalk table, and he was just a few yards up from where we were on the shady (read "cold") side of the street. There wasn't anything on his table except a big jar and a sign that read: **"Raffle! Win a First Edition of Silence of the Lambs."** In order to enter, passersby had to leave a business card or other name-and-address information in the jar. Instant mailing list.

Directly behind the table was the storefront that was going to be Doug's shop. It was narrow, only about fifteen feet wide. The door was in the middle, with a tall display window on either side. On the window to the left of the door was painted:

**Printers
Row Fine
& Rare
BOOKS**

Doug had put some makeshift display racks inside both windows and had arranged a few of his books across the front. It wasn't a large selection—there were only about twenty or thirty books in all—but it was remarkably choice. He had first editions of *The Natural*, *The Great Gatsby* (the dust jacket looked almost new and we wondered if it was *the* copy), *The Beautiful and Damned* (in a fantastic dust jacket with a drawing of two obviously young and spoiled rich people), *Pulp* by Charles Bukowski, *The Big Sleep*, *The Grapes of Wrath*, *The Hound of the Baskervilles* (no dust jacket but we're not sure it came with one), *Madame Bovary*, *A Farewell to Arms*, *On the Road* (an excellent copy that Doug was selling for two thousand dollars—sixteen hundred dollars less than Crawford Doyle was asking for a copy in no better and possibly not as good condition), *Death in the Afternoon*, *Atlas Shrugged*, and *A Confederacy of Dunces*.

After we introduced ourselves, Doug took us over to the window to discuss some of the books. We asked immediately about the *Gatsby*.

"No," he said quietly, "that's not it. I had to put the *Gatsby* in a facsimile dust jacket. I was afraid to bring the first-issue dust jacket here. The security system isn't in yet. I have the real jacket at home."

Too bad. He needn't have worried, though. He obviously didn't know about the on-duty sergeant hulking through the crowd, intimidating potential evildoers and cowardly bibliophiles alike.

Doug asked us to come inside and see the shop, but just before he turned the key in the lock, another couple walked up. They looked successful and seemed to be in their forties or early fifties. The man was wearing a crisply ironed silk safari shirt and the woman was in a denim ensemble, which, from its dark blue patina, had only ever been dry cleaned. We had noticed them earlier. They seemed to have arrived at about the same time we had and had taken a similar path down Dearborn. They stood out because they had seemed much more serious in their browsing than most of the other fair-goers.

The man started pointing to books in the window and asking their prices. Every time Doug told him, the man nodded perfunctorily and said he wanted it. He never asked to touch the books or even see them on the inside. When Doug told him about the facsimile dust jacket on the *Gatsby,* and said that the actual book was over thirty thousand dollars, the man just nodded once more. The woman never said a word.

At that point, the man asked Doug if he and his wife might come inside. Doug waved for us to come in as well. Although we did, it was not without trepidation. We are not as trusting as Doug. Each of us, as we confirmed later, felt certain that the second the door was closed and locked behind us, the man, or more likely his wife, would pull out a concealed weapon and that we would then have the truly unique bibliophilic experience of watching Doug's stock stuffed into a plastic garbage bag before it disappeared out the back door. Perhaps we would be shot as well.

But that is why Doug Phillips is a book dealer and we are not. All the man wanted to do, it turned out, was to question Doug about what else he had in his stock. When he was done, we heard him say, "I can't do this now. Call me on Monday."

After they were gone and the door was again locked behind them, Doug came over and showed us a page on a legal pad. He had a funny look on his face.

"He wants to buy a *lot* of books."

"Is he a dealer?"

"No," said Doug, "a collector."

"That's a pretty good first day," we noted, since one of the books was the *Gatsby.*

"Do you think he's for real?" Doug asked.

"Who knows? You'll find out on Monday."

Then Doug showed us around. The shop wasn't close to being done yet. The shelves had just been varnished and were set out to dry on a drop cloth set over the cases in the center of the room. There were some very neat power tools on a sawhorse table just in front of that. But there was no doubt from the little that had already been done that this was going to be a beautiful shop—not grand, but warm and inviting. It had hardwood floors and a fireplace. Shelf units ran along one wall of the shop. They were painted forest green and outlined in sienna with leaded deco glass doors ornamented with tulips. We asked Doug if he had had the doors made specially.

"No," he said. "I got them at a salvage furniture place. They told me the stained glass came from a monastery."

On the other side of the shop stood an eight-foot-tall, fifteen-foot-wide oak cabinet with large glass-fronted shelves, the whole thing balanced on several pairs of skinny oak legs. "This one came from a reform school," said Doug. "I'm not sure what they used it for."

He gestured toward the drop cloth–covered cases with the drying shelves on top. "These are from a 1920s jewelry shop. I'm going to use them for the library tables," he continued. "And come back here and see this."

He led us to the back of the shop and to a small anteroom. Tucked in the corner was a six-foot-high, several-ton, old-fashioned iron safe.

"It's from the 1890s," said Doug. "At one time, this was a printer's shop. I'd love to get the safe out of here and into the front room and use it as a bookcase, but it's incredibly heavy. If this place was hit by a bomb, the only thing left standing at the end would be this safe."

"A printer's office, huh? That's fitting. Was that what it was before you took it over?"

"No," said Doug. "It was a dentist's office until about three weeks ago."

As we were leaving, Doug said, "I know I'm going against the current. I was just speaking this morning to someone whose store closed in Oak Park. It's sort of discouraging. I know I need an Internet presence and I'm going to have one. But I really want to do this."

He unlocked the front door. "Have a great time at the fair. I've found some really terrific stuff here over the years. There's no better feeling than combing through piles of books and finding a diamond in the rough."

But when we were back on the street, it wasn't diamonds we suddenly craved, but lunch. We had been hit by the powerful and distinctive aroma of sautéed garlic. We followed the smell into a large, bookless tent where about fifty folding chairs had been set up facing a raised platform on which a chef named Jason Handelman, from the Park Avenue Café (with locations in New York and Chicago), was preparing Tomato Curry with Black Mussels for Potato Crusted Halibut on portable burners. It was part of an ongoing string of cooking demonstrations by local chefs. There was quite a crowd gathered to watch Jason (who was tall and very good-looking in his white double-breasted chef's jacket) and we got there just in time to catch him making the sauce.

He suggested that the audience follow along by helping themselves to copies of the recipe, a stack of which were sitting on the front table. In the spirit of authenticity, we've decided to pass it along. (By the way, Jason was very firm in noting that one should make sure the mustard seeds pop before turning the heat down.)

Tomato Curry with Black Mussels
for Potato Crusted Halibut
(serves 8)

½ tsp. mustard seeds
¼ tsp. cumin seeds
1 tbsp. vegetable oil
½ tsp. minced garlic
½ tsp. minced ginger
2 c. tomatoes—finely chopped & seeded
½ tsp. ground red pepper (cayenne)
⅛ tsp. ground turmeric

1 tsp. salt
1 tsp. lemon juice
20 pc. mussels—steamed & removed from shell
pickled cilantro (optional)

In a covered medium frying pan, heat mustard and cumin seeds over medium heat. When mustard seeds begin to pop, turn heat down to low. Add garlic and ginger—stir for 30 seconds. Add tomatoes and simmer for 2–3 minutes. Add red pepper, turmeric and salt. Cook until tomatoes start to break up. Add steamed mussels and lemon juice. Garnish with pickled cilantro (optional).

8 6oz. pieces halibut
2 large potatoes
¼ cup butter (melted)

Potato crust: Cut 2 potato cylinders out of 2 whole potatoes by cutting the potatoes with a small piece of pipe. Boil the potato cylinders in salted water until they are ¾ cooked—do not fully cook the potatoes. Cool potatoes. Slice potato cylinders across to get little circles of potato about ⅛" thick. Layer the potatoes on top of fish filets to resemble fish scales. Cover layered potatoes with melted butter and cool so butter hardens and keeps potatoes in place. To cook: Place fish, potato side down, over medium heat in fry pan. Cook until potatoes are crispy then turn filet and cook fully in oven at 350 degrees for five minutes.

Lacking a piece of clean pipe, as of this writing we have yet to try this recipe. However, we would welcome comments from any of our readers intrepid enough to do so. We can say that it smelled great and, after leaving the cooking tent, we immediately repaired to the local Thai restaurant.

On the way back to the car, we stopped one last time at a booth at which we may or may not have stopped previously. We were lingering actually, almost depleted of cash and pretty sure we had seen everything, but still somehow not wanting to leave. Then, on the top shelf, we saw Lowell Thomas's *With Lawrence in Arabia.*

We had recently introduced Emily to *Lawrence of Arabia,* which has one of the all-time great screenplays. ("Akaba is over there, it is only a matter of going." "He lied. He is not perfect." "With Colonel Lawrence, mercy is a passion. With me, it is merely good manners. I leave it to you to choose which motive is the more . . . reliable." "A man like me who tells lies merely hides the truth. A man who tells half-lies has forgotten where he put it.")

Lowell Thomas, of course, was the American reporter—Chicago based, we believe—whose articles helped make T. E. Lawrence a hero. ("You have a story you want told and I badly need a story to tell," Arthur Kennedy as the Thomas character tells Alec Guinness as Prince Feisal.) We didn't have *With Lawrence in Arabia,* so we pulled the book out to take a look.

It was a Grosset & Dunlap 1921 reprint in decent condition. The dust jacket had a drawing of Lawrence in Arab costume, standing in the desert with camels and Arab soldiers behind him. This was the real T. E. Lawrence, who was five-foot-three and looked nothing like Peter O'Toole. (The latter had prompted Noël Coward, as he was walking out of the premiere of the film, to observe, "If he had been any prettier, he'd be Florence of Arabia.") The book lacked the photographs of the more expensive editions, but at $9.95 (on sale for $7) it seemed the perfect cap to the day.

Just before we got to our car, on the corner but out of the fair area itself, a woman was handing out leaflets. She held one our way and said something earnestly that we couldn't quite make out. Thinking that this was another book promotion, we took the leaflet. Across the top it read:

Tap Water Kills More People
Than Guns

We called Doug Phillips after we got home to find out about his customer.

"He seems to be genuine," Doug told us. "He's interested in about twelve books to start with, but he said he would buy more later on. They were mostly the books I put in the window. I gave him the prices and he said he'd talk it over with his wife and get back to me."

Twelve wasn't one hundred but still a pretty good way to kick off the shop. "And who won the raffle?"

"Oh," said Doug, "it was a philosophy professor at the University of Chicago. He was interested in Kant and Hegel and that kind of thing. I had a few of those. I'm not sure he's a *Silence of the Lambs* kind of person, but it's his now."

Chapter 7

AFTERWORD

We thought, to close, we might include a few outtakes. While we were doing the chapter on the New England forger, we were curious as to what was going to happen to all those Kenneth Anderson books. John Crichton told us that the ABAA was making an effort to have any of its members who might still have Anderson books forward them to him, so that they could be permanently sequestered. Although many dealers complied, John, as we noted, was meeting with staunch resistance from some others, who were reluctant (or outright refused) to part with Anderson books.

We remembered that Peter Stern had told us that these forgeries would be surfacing for years, so, we wondered, how easy was it to obtain an Anderson book?

We decided to try and buy the book that had gotten the whole thing started, the double-signed *Passages from the Letters of John Butler Yeats: Selected by Ezra Pound*. It was a good test case and besides, we thought it would be a neat book to have as a memento in our collection. (We even debated briefly whether or not, if we could actually secure the book, to ask Ken Anderson to sign it as well.)

Terry Halladay had told us that, soon after the signatures had been identified as forgeries, *Passages* had been returned to Bradford's. When we called Bradford's, they were understandably disinclined to discuss the matter, but finally they told us that they, in turn, had sent the book back to Randy Weinstein, the dealer who had originally consigned them the book.

"It's in a box in the garage," Randy told us when we called him. "I don't know what I'm going to do with it."

We suggested that he sell it to us.

"But the signatures are fakes," he said. "Why do you want it?"

"Well, who knows," we replied, "maybe someday Anderson forgeries might have some value of their own."

Randy agreed that this might be the case. (When we expressed that view to another dealer, he said, "Nah. Anderson forgeries won't be worth anything. There're too many of them.")

We asked Randy how much he wanted for it.

"Oh, I don't know. Fifty dollars?"

We agreed and, within a week, the book was in our hands. We first looked at the razored-out front endpaper, where, we surmised, the Kenneth R. Anderson blind stamp had once been, and then opened to the colophon to check out what Terry and Jim Lowe had said about the signatures against the actual object.

We're no experts, and certainly if we'd seen the book at a fair being sold by a reputable dealer, we wouldn't have questioned it, but looking at the "W. B. Yeats" and the "Ezra Pound," we were amazed that this could have fooled anyone who knew anything. Not only was it obvious that both signatures had been done with the same pen, they looked like the same handwriting . . . same size, same spacing, even the same general shape of the letters. Was it possible, we wondered, that if this book had fallen into the hands of less-reputable dealers than Jim Cummins and Terry Halladay, it actually would have ended up in someone's collection?

There was something else. This book was one of four hundred printed. Certainly, far fewer than that survive. It is a piece of history

Here ends 'Passages from the Letters of John Butler Yeats,' selected by Ezra Pound. Published and printed by Elizabeth Corbet Yeats on paper made in Ireland, at the Cuala Press, Churchtown, Dundrum, in the County of Dublin, Ireland. Finished in the last week of February, nineteen hundred and seventeen.

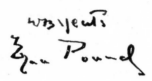

and Ken Anderson, by defacing the book as he did, destroyed that history. A number of dealers we had spoken to had expressed this same sentiment, but it was only when we held the book in our hands that we felt it too.

We were asked to be the speakers at a private library in Manhattan to kick off their annual book sale. They seemed genuinely excited about having us, which was very flattering. (They even paid us, which was more flattering still.) It was a cold, rainy, particularly revolting day but, still, about fifty people showed up, which filled every seat and left some people standing on the side.

Everything went very well. We started with the worst book-signing story ever and found out that someone in the audience was actually a friend of George Dawes Green. (We asked him later if he knew whether or not the story was true, and he said, "I don't know, but that's the kind of thing that always happens to George.") We went on about how we got started collecting, including the famous dropping-the-tree-on-the-house story—which we can still tell since it is one of the few events in our marriage that we have yet to put in a book—then read the first pages of the New England forger chapter and talked about on-line bookselling.

After we had finished, the audience was enthusiastic, asking questions for over twenty minutes. Most of the questions concerned our views of the Internet and the forger, but toward the end, one woman asked, "What do you think of mystery writers . . . like Lawrence Block, for instance?"

Before we could answer, a woman yelled from the back, "WE DIDN'T HEAR THE QUESTION!"

"THE QUESTION WAS, 'WHAT DO YOU THINK OF LAWRENCE BLOCK?'" replied one of us, the pushy one who is always unfairly accused of interrupting his wife.

"THANK YOU," yelled the woman.

"LAWRENCE BLOCK . . ." the pushy one continued, continuing to speak at top volume to make sure that every person in the audience could hear. "WELL, I TEND TO READ MYSTERY WRITERS AT THE BEGINNING OF THEIR CAREERS. IT'S A DIFFICULT GENRE IN WHICH TO STAY FRESH. MOST MYSTERY WRITERS GET A LITTLE STALE OVER TIME AND THE LATER WORK CAN FALL OFF QUITE A BIT."

Then the other of us told how difficult it had been for her to write her first mystery and how she marveled at mystery writers who seemed to be able to turn out a book a year, sometimes more.

After we had finished, the director walked over and said, "Lawrence Block was in the audience, you know."

"Oh, God."

"The woman who asked the question didn't realize he was here. He's a major supporter of the library."

"Oy."

"Oh, that's all right," said the director reassuringly. "He'd probably agree with you."

Sure.

"He didn't look unhappy when he left," the director went on.

On the other hand, he didn't come up and introduce himself either.

We get a lot of mail. Most of it is complimentary. There's even a man in Texas, obviously someone of great literary discernment, who jokes about being president of our fan club. (Thank you, M. W.) Some of the mail is not so wonderful. We've been taken to task for bad writing, bad language, and bad scholarship. Occasionally, someone writes to tell us that he or she is sick of our discussions of where we eat when we go book hunting. We don't pay much attention to these—anyone who doesn't appreciate the intimate link between books and food is obviously not a genuine bibliophile.

There was one letter, however, that stands out in that it seems to sum up the frustration of every author (including us) who tries in vain to get his or her book out there, in the front rack at Barnes & Noble or Borders, where casual buyers can snatch them up by the armload.

In the first chapter of *Slightly Chipped,* we recounted our visit to Boston just after our first book, *Used and Rare,* had come out (thus getting the titles of both books in the same sentence), and our inability to find a copy anywhere until we went to Waterstones on Exeter Street and found out they had stuck it alllll the way in the back of the store in "Literary Criticism"—a section that the salesperson helpfully referred to as "the garbage dump of the store."

About six months later, we got this letter from a woman in Wichita, Kansas:

> I very much enjoyed your newest book, *Slightly Chipped: Footnotes in Booklore.*
> The first few pages of chapter one, in which you recount your search for *Used and Rare* in a bookstore, gave me a great deal of amusement. I had browsed through *Slightly Chipped* in the new arrivals section of my local

Barnes and Noble and decided, since I'd already spent more than I'd planned, to purchase it on a future visit.

However, when that day arrived I incorrectly recalled your names and had totally forgotten the title. All I knew was that I wanted a book on books by the Gold-somethings. It wasn't in the "books on books" section, nor in reference, nor in literary criticism. . . . By that time I was absolutely determined, but to no avail.

The week before Christmas I found it while looking for a gift—in the home improvement section!

Of all the misfilings we've experienced as authors, this one confused us the most. Then, finally, we got it. Whoever had filed the book had ignored the subtitle and decided that "Slightly Chipped" must refer to furniture.

Right after we had finished speaking at BookMania!, we were walking to our car in the parking lot when we were approached by a huge, burly man with long, wild hair and a tattoo on his arm whom we had seen loitering around the Blake Library. He was wearing a T-shirt, old jeans, and boots. Everything was there but the big Harley. He looked *baaad*. He stopped right in front of us, barring our way.

Uh-oh, maybe not everyone there had liked our performance after all.

Then the man stuck out his hand.

"Hi," he said. "My name's Anthony Watkins. I'm sorry I missed your talk. I was helping out. I do a little bit of everything . . . construction, publicity . . . whatever they need."

"Are you a book collector?"

He shook his head. "A poet," he said and then handed us a copy of a small newspaper from a stack that he was carrying. Across the top, it read:

**Winter 2000—Poetry, Poetry & More
Price:
1 New Thought**
Abundance
A HARVEST OF LIFE, LITERATURE & ART

"I'm the publisher," he said.

The paper was sixteen pages long. In addition to selections from local poets, there were articles, movie reviews, cartoons, a calendar of local events in the arts, classifieds, ads from a diverse group of local merchants, including an auto dealer, a frame shop, a pizzeria, and a couple of bars, and, on page two, a vitriolic editorial that covered everything from gay and animal rights to the secret desire of many police officers to beat confessions out of suspects. And oh, yes, on the front page there was an interview with the tall, good-looking, ex-football player Ace Atkins (the man was everywhere).

"I've written poetry since I was a kid," said Anthony. "I was amazed that you could make poems."

Anthony Watkins grew up in Alabama. His father owned a greenhouse, and then started a construction company. When it was time for college, Anthony went to Auburn, starting out in engineering school.

"I was a sophomore at seventeen," he said. "I was still a sophomore at twenty, so I dropped out."

After college, Anthony trained as an EMT, sold cars, and worked as a salesman for Pepsi Cola. Now, he works for his father, who has also moved to Florida but still owns a construction company. "I remodel bathrooms in Palm Beach County."

He started the newsletter in October 1995. "I did it with my wife at the time. After the first issue, my wife moved on from both me and the paper." He kept the operation going. "I used to call it 'Art Scene,' and it was pretty much a straight newsletter. I started with a run of about five thousand. It grew pretty well, to about fifteen thousand circulation. But then I started getting more subversive, more political. Circulation shrunk back to where it was when I started but we're starting to grow again."

Even though his father thinks of *Abundance* as an "expensive hobby," he allows Anthony's schedule to be flexible enough to get the paper out. "I tried to explain to him that I only do the bathrooms to support the paper," he said. "There are a lot of artists in the area and most of them are very approachable. Artistically, this is the most exciting place I've ever lived. You know, we put out our five thousand copies and they always disappear—when they're gone, people ask where they are.

"There's a sports bar called Roosters—they have karaoke Friday nights, to give you an idea. We used to leave about fifty papers. Now, a sports bar with karaoke is the last place you'd think a poetry newsletter is going to work. Well, the fifty papers always used to disappear. And they weren't just throwing them out either. When I came in one day, they said a lot of people couldn't get them, so could I start leaving sixty."

We go to the New York Antiquarian Book Fair every year. It's $12 a person to get in, but we generally manage to buy at least one book there, and we make it a matter of pride to try and find the cheapest thing in the joint. (The $175 copy of *Rossetti and His Circle* was the exception but, since we've subsequently seen copies not as good as ours sell for over $300, we're not going to complain.)

But mostly we go because, for book theater, it is the best show anywhere.

This year, we hadn't been inside for more than thirty seconds when we came upon the booth of B&L Rootenberg Rare Books of Sherman Oaks, California. There, in front of their display, was an open case on a table with a lot of little, round marblelike objects, each with a little blue or brown colored circle in the middle. It was, in fact:

ARTIFICIAL HUMAN EYES
English (ca. 1860.) A set of 100 glass eyes of varying colours contained in the original box, each in its own velvet-lined compart-
ment. These eyes were used by the doctor as models for fitting a
patient who had lost an eye.

$5000.00

The eyes were not set in their little velvet-lined compartments
in any particular way and so seemed to be looking off in every direction at once. The ones staring right at us seemed to be doing so
with an accusing air.

As we wandered up and down the aisles, we saw a copy of the
Augsburg Confession, which was presented to Charles V in 1530. It
was a small volume, bound in white leather, in remarkably good
condition, selling for $20,000. Just a few feet away, there was a map
of colonial Virginia, with a drawing of Powhatan in the corner, for
$7,500.

As always, modern firsts were everywhere. We saw an absolutely perfect copy of *The Hamlet* for $6,500, a decent copy of
The Maltese Falcon for $18,000, and, at Nick Adams & Co Rare
Books, there were three typed manuscripts, parts 1, 2, and 3 of Don
DeLillo's *Underworld,* selling for $375. They were among twenty
copies the publisher produced as the first advance printing for its
salesmen.

With all the fair's riches, however, nothing prepared us for what
we saw when we came to Peter Harrington, Antiquarian Bookseller, one of the many dealers who had come to New York from
the UK to exhibit at this fair.

In their glass display case were three books, the titles of which
are known to every parent in America, but whose dust jackets are
rarely seen here.

"How much are they?" we asked. "Someone told us that the set
was selling for $17,500."

"Oh, no," said the man behind the case. He was young, hip, and handsome. UK dealers seem to specialize in employees who look like they could make a quick transition to the movies. "That's only for the first one. And it's in pounds."

"Pounds?"

"Oh, yes. In dollars, it's twenty-four thousand five."

"Twenty-four thousand five for Harry Potter?" we asked, even more aghast than we had been when Mark Samuels Lasner had given us the previous astronomic figure.

"The first UK is a very rare book," said the man. "They only printed three hundred copies in hardcover, you see, and most of those went to school libraries. Other than the author's copies, there are almost none left that don't have library stamps all over them."

If J. K. Rowling had gotten the twenty-five hardcovers that most authors get, that meant, in addition to everything else she's made on Harry Potter, she was sitting on an additional $600,000 in first editions. And if she *signed* them . . .

"The second one is forty-eight hundred dollars," the man went on, "and the third is only eight hundred. The fourth one won't be worth much more than retail. There were two hundred paperback proofs of the first book also, by the way. They are even harder to find than a hardcover."

When we stopped by the Brick Row Books booth to speak with John Crichton, the first topic that came up, of course, was Kenneth Anderson.

"Nobody's received a penny of restitution yet," said John, "at least nothing beyond what was taken in from the sale of his books. People are grumbling, but I think it's just a bureaucratic issue, rather than something on Anderson's part."

After researching Anderson and Max, we also wanted to meet Ed Maggs (he was the antiquarian bookseller who was at the British Museum for the Enoch Soames celebration). We asked a man at the Maggs booth if Ed was there.

"No," replied the man, "he just stepped away. He'll probably be back soon, though. We just got him some coffee."

"We'll come back in a little while," we said. "Maybe we'll see him on the floor. What does he look like?"

"Like John Cleese," said another Maggs employee.

We stared for a moment, wondering whether to ask.

"No," said the first man, "he doesn't have a silly walk."

When we came back, Ed had returned. He was tall, with a mustache. He didn't actually look like John Cleese, but there was a twinkle in his manner that bespoke a potential Cleesian sense of humor.

Ed, as it turned out, was head of the Max Beerbohm Society, of which there were four other official members and about 250 hangers-on.

"The Beerbohm Society didn't take any organization," Ed told us. "It just kind of happened. We had a couple of meetings in pubs."

A little later on, we ran into our old friend John Sanderson. He asked us if we were working on another book and we told him that we were.

"How can I get in this one? I already used the 'I want to play myself in the movie' line."

"Well, what did you bring with you?"

Sure enough, John got us again. Here is a sampling of his books: *Diseases of the Tongue*; *The Art of Preserving the Hair*; also, *The Loss of Hair*; a book on fitting dentures filled with extremely explicit (and disgusting) photographs; *Animals for Show and Pleasure in Ancient Rome*; *The Gypsies and Detectives*; and, last but not least, that old favorite, *The Biochemistry of Semen*.

We came across another dealer we knew from the Berkshires and the conversation, as it always does, went from books to the weather.

"We got six inches of snow over the weekend," said the dealer. "It melted quickly but it was the wet, sloppy kind. One day we had daffodils and tulips and the next day they were dead."

"We try to grow tulips every year," we said. "But just before the buds open, the deer come along and eat them. We've tried all these things that people tell us to spray that the deer don't like, but nothing works."

"Oh," said the dealer, "haven't you tried urine?"

"Urine? As in pee?"

"Sure. The deer hate the smell of human urine. I just go out with my squeeze bottle every time after it rains. We have lots of deer and I never lose any tulips."

Without giving away any identities here, suffice it to say that this dealer was not a person we previously would have imagined peeing into a squeeze bottle then going around and spritzing the contents on flowers. Of course, in the world of used and antiquarian books, if you hang around long enough, you'll run into just about everything.

Oh, yes. We are sorry to have to report that Wilkins lost in a runoff.